D1060258

MATURATION OF THE THERAPEUTIC COMMUNITY

Community Mental Health Series

Research Contributions from Psychology to Community Mental Health
J.W. Carter, Jr., Ph.D.

Coordinate Index Reference Guide to Community Mental Health
S.E. Golann, Ph.D.

Mental Health and the Community
M.F. Shore, Ph.D. and F.V. Mannino, Ph.D.

Task Force on Community Mental Health, Division 27
American Psychological Association, Issues in
Community Psychology and Preventive Mental Health

The Critical Issues in Community Mental Health
H. Gottesfeld, Ph.D.

Behavioral Threat and Community Response
W. Rhodes, Ph.D.

Support Systems and Community Mental Health: Lectures on Concept Development
G. Caplan, M.D.

Challenge to Community Psychiatry
A.R. Foley, M.D.

The Therapeutic Community
J.J. Rossi Ph.D. and W.J. Filstead, Ph.D.

Community Psychology and Social Systems
S. Murrell, Ph. D.

Changing Patterns of Psychiatric Care
B.L. Bloom, Ph.D.

Current and Future Trends in Community Psychology
S.E. Golann, Ph.D. and J. Baker

Consultation-Education: Development and Evaluation
C.D. Vacher, Ph.D. and N.E. Stratas, M.D.

Maturation of the Therapeutic Community: An Organic Approach to Health and Mental Health
M. Jones, M.D.

MATURATION OF THE THERAPEUTIC COMMUNITY

An Organic Approach to Health and Mental Health

Maxwell Jones, M.D.

Library of Congress Catalog Number 75-11002

ISBN: 0-87705-264-6

Printed in the United States of America
6789 987654321

To :

Greta, Lisa, & Anna

About the author:

Rebelling against the orthodoxy of medicine and psychiatry at an early age, the author has spent nearly thirty years in developing social organizations which promote social learning and growth in their members. Originating in a setting of psychiatric hospitals, the concepts of a therapeutic community were evolved. This led to involvement with other institutions such as prisons and schools, where an attempt was made to change from a closed (hierarchical) system to a more open or democratic social organization. Dr. Jones believes that only in this way can the latent potential in every individual be developed. But this calls for a revolution in the social organization of schools and of education generally. All individuals and all systems tend to resist change but a methodology for change is emerging. Will society risk such a choice, or remain bound to conformity and material values of status, money, and power?

CONTENTS

FOREWORD

This book primarily examines the concept of the open system as it applies to health. An open system is perhaps best understood in terms of its opposite. A closed system is only too familiar to us all. Our schooling has almost invariably included one-way communication (teaching rather than learning)—a passive receptive role for the pupil, relatively little sharing of information (subject matter only, e.g., math, science, etc.), no significant responsibility to one's peers or to the school, an absence of shared decision making or of learning as a social process.

Open systems are "open" in respect to the environment. Thus, in an open school frequent opportunities arise for interaction between pupil and teacher, pupil and pupil, or spontaneously formed groups around common interests, e.g., building a model aircraft. Such a topic draws on the information contained in the group, and initiates a process of learning. To have an effective outcome, such a group task calls for shared decision making and a feeling of shared responsibility.

My experience of social systems has been mainly in psychiatric settings—hospitals, clinics, etc., in schools or in prisons. Size has been of fundamental importance because the system must allow numerous face-to-face contacts with everyone in the system, so for me a system means an upper limit of approximately 100 people. Above that arbitrary figure we need some form of representation for the various subgroups or a decentralization plan, with semiautonomous units.

The trouble with such a concept of a social system is that in many hospitals, schools, or correctional institutions the staff will number less than 100 but the consumers will be much more numerous. The temptation to develop a highly integrated staff and to forget the consumer is strong.

Even if the system includes the consumer, as in a psychiatric ward, a school classroom, or a correctional unit, new difficulties arise at the interface with the larger system of the parent body.

Given such a relatively circumscribed and visible social system, then we can attempt to identify some of the qualities and study the effects of such a systems approach to social change.

Perhaps the greatest difficulty in writing this book has been a medical bias. The training for an M.D. and the equally long training in formal psychiatry inevitably conditions one to look for pathology. But even the man in the street seems to be much more interested in illness than in health. Illness happens as "an act of God" and even psychiatric illness seems commonly to be given this quality of inevitability.

It seems to me that to focus on health as opposed to illness, calls for a much higher degree of involvement by the individuals comprising the system. In the latter, the medical system is the active agent and the individual is in varying degrees the passive recipient of treatment. Admittedly, this is changing in family therapy and crisis intervention techniques, but the psychopathology and the symptoms are still the focal point for change, and the medical terms are the prime movers in treatment.

Without the focus of removing or modifying pathology we have to introduce new goals for change. The fear of death through physical illness and suicide or madness through mental illness have a universal quality, calling for help in a way that other crises in society cannot match. The crisis of a war or violence strike fear into most ordinary individuals, but the fear is ultimately of death, disease, or mental suffering.

At the present time, change agents (consultants with a professional background, or facilitators) are invoked with increasing frequency by business firms, schools, and other agencies. Their function is invariably related to some problem, invented or real, which calls for intervention. The interventionist attempts to collect valid information, identify the problem or problems, and help the system to resolve its difficulties.

In this situation the interventionist is not a medical doctor but probably a behavioral scientist. We have moved from the field of pathology and medicine to the field of social problems and psychology.

Can we hope to move further along this continuum to explore such possibilities as restructuring society in an attempt to meet the problems of a technological age—rapid change in consumer needs; uneven distribution of basic necessities like food, contraception, education, thoughtless waste of natural resources leading to a world shortage; pollution and ecological disaster?

Here the urgency and personal anxiety may be absent in a large section of society. People, in general, have not learned to identify themselves with larger social units than perhaps the home or their own particular peer group. The famine in India seems very far away, and anyway, the first concern is for the self or one's immediate family.

To be a change agent in these wider problem areas is to court disaster. Who knows what directions society must take in order to protect itself from extinction? In any case these global problems are the concern of rational governments. Behind these valid rationalizations lurks the most basic problem of all—man's almost universal resistance to change as an ongoing process. The advent of radio and

T.V. may change patterns of leisure, but this is a passive acceptance of change that makes one's amusement available by turning a switch; it has none of the personal involvement required by planned activities that demand personal effort.

It is my contention that health, in the full sense of the term, implies realizing the potential for growth in every individual. The growth process is, or should be, the concern of the mother and her family system in the newborn child. The responsibility for the infant and child is shared by the family, school, peer group, etc. Ever-widening systems impinge on the adolescent and the adult.

In the past, the tendency has been to identify individual problems only when symptoms of illness (physical or mental) appear. Little or no attention was paid to the potentially illness-producing environment. Systems theory has a population focus and raises the possibility that not only the prevention of illness, but the promotion of health and psychosocial growth may be enhanced.

It may be premature to visualize such a health-producing environment. The skills needed for such a transformation of existing social organizations do not yet exist, although a beginning has been made.[1]

In the final analysis it may be that mankind has neither the inclination nor the capacity to change toward planned goals. If change in the direction of a health-producing environment for everyone is to become possible, the educational system would seem to have the greatest potential to promote this.

The open system concept already has a place in the school system in the form of open schools. This trend is arousing tremendous interest and controversy. These ex-

[1]Perhaps the best position statement to date is by Stanley A. Murrell, *Community Psychology and Social Systems* (New York: Behavioral Publications, 1973).

perimental beginnings are found mainly in the elementary schools. Children moving from such open schools to the more traditional, relatively closed junior high or high schools are inevitably affected by the conformist environment. Even if one county school district or state authority could evolve an open system throughout the child's education, if possible continued at the state university, we would at least have a pilot project.

To attempt an educational program with the parents at the same time might be impracticable. But the children exposed to such open systems would themselves become parents in most instances, and in three or four generations the social environment might at least have a greater emphasis on health and psychosocial growth.

This grossly oversimplified schema will be elaborated further in this book. Experience to date justifies optimism, in my opinion. The major stumbling block appears to be man's resistance to change once he has established his identity in his school years and has formulated his goals at work. The usual goals of financial success and status, with their implied competitiveness, have deep ego rewards for most people in the so-called progressive countries.

The concepts of an open system applied from the earliest years might, in time, result in adults who have mastered problem-solving skills, and have trusting and supportive peer group relationships that would continually evaluate their social values and have a positive effect on health and self-fulfillment.

In this book the focus is largely on the behavioral model of social organization, favored by the behavioral scientists. The implication is, despite an effort to be open-minded, that this approach is preferable to the classical or bureaucratic hierarchical model favored by much of big business. To deny such a bias would be dishonest. The fact that the concern is primarily with human health and self-fulfillment is sufficient justification for this value judgment.

The goals of an organization will inevitably be an important factor in determining its social structure. Thus, the business world will, of necessity, have profit as a top priority, and this is linked to a central control in which the manager organizes the system into specialized departments operating under chosen leaders. He determines objectives and deadlines that determine standards of performance, and information is fed back to him at the central control. This is the classical hierarchical or pyramidal model with a tendency toward one-way communication, unilateral decision making, and a passive, recipient role for the workers.

However, even in the business world, things are changing in response to the rapidly changing world. New technology calls for new methods of production, which in turn call for a new social organization. Circumstances such as these place new strains on workers and force managements to pay increasing attention to human relations in industry. Such considerations may weigh less heavily in a stable industry, such as steel, compared to the conditions of uncertainty and flux that characterize the computer industry. Nevertheless, many other factors, such as the overall higher level of education, reaction to boredom in repetitive work, the new climate of freedom from restraint that characterizes much of American youth and is linked with a need to experience job satisfaction, all force management to reconsider the human factor in industry. This need to consider employee satisfaction has persuaded a minority of employers to adopt at least some of the aspects of a democratic horizontal system with lessening of controls, greater diffusion of responsibility and authority, and shared decision making.

Various compromises between the extremes of the hierarchical and the behavioral models are emerging. Thus, what has been called the integrating position is an attempt to reconcile the above two models and blend the efficiency and control of the one with the relative freedom from control and humanistic approach of the other.

The organic model of social organization argues that the classical hierarchical model is too rigid to adapt to the rapidly changing world brought about by modern technology. To meet these changes, temporary task forces made up of relative strangers who possess the relevant skills to solve the immediate problem will be formed. "The groups will be conducted on organic rather than on mechanical lines; they will emerge and adapt to the problems, and leadership and influence will fall to those who seem most able to solve the problems, rather than according to the programmed role expectations. People will be differentiated, not according to rank of roles, but according to skills and training."[2]

Many other models of social organization in industry have been described, but as yet no one approach has won general acceptance as a workable systems approach to organization. But there is a growing body of evidence to indicate that increased production and job satisfaction for employees are directly related to each other.

We have discussed industrial organizations partly because most people are involved in such systems and because these systems have been studied most extensively to date. However, our concern in this book is primarily with health; school and family systems have much greater significance for positive health programs than industry.

One feels that the long-term goal for a healthy society is to help the growing child to think for himself, learn to identify and solve problems as they arise, interact with his peers, parents, and teachers in an open and informal way that enhances the process of learning, and enjoy the free-

[2]Warren G. Bennis, *Organization Development: Its Nature, Origins, and Prospects* (Reading, Mass.: Addison-Wesley, 1969).

dom to choose his own value system. It is for this reason that an attempt has been made to link clinical experience and the hospital "sickness model," with a preventative health program identified with schools and families.

INTRODUCTION

During the last decade psychiatry, like society itself, has had to re-examine its function and goals. Does it contribute significantly to people's happiness? Can it meet the challenge of our times, when technology is changing the role of man at a rate unprecedented in our history? Is it still largely a luxury, claiming to enhance the dreams of self-fulfillment that are or were part of the middle class culture, particularly in the United States? For a time the followers of Freud understandably believed that such dreams were near to fulfillment, at least for many people. But they failed to take full cognizance of dimensions of living other than the intrapsychic—the pressures of everyday living that might be related to infantile traumata, but that operated independently too: the cultural revolution (dare we say evolution?) that questioned most or all of our established values, and that on the surface at least gave promise of a new working model. Religion, one of the mainstays of our value system in the past, has lost much of its significance in the present. The uncertainty of the Church of Rome at this time of soul searching, and its failure to give a clear message to a confused world, is symptomatic of our current dilemma. Its very failure as viewed by many thinking people may be to its credit; at least there are signs that even in this most traditional of organizations there is a conscious need for rethinking and reassessing values and beliefs.

In the business field there is less evidence of concern over human values. In this relatively material world the goals can be made more explicit. The profit motive transcends all and is relatively available to mathematical analysis. Even though behavioral scientists are invading this field as consultants, they are there to facilitate the goals of industry, which in terms of profit and loss are relatively simple. Human values are important when considering morale, but the human element has a hard struggle becoming visible or articulate in the large impersonal organizations of our time. Only where it impinges on the material goals of industry is the concept of an open system tolerated.[1] The open system even if adopted is limited only to learning, sharing, and interacting on matters relevant to industrial growth and the needs of stockholders. The power structure may be discussed in this context and some changes effected in the direction of greater sharing of responsibility and authority, but these role changes may have little or no effect on the lives of the majority of employees (the workers), apart from a possibly larger pay packet. In other words, the goals in industrial organizations are material, and few if any people as yet expect them to include the "pursuit of happiness."

In the political field, similar priorities seem to predominate, particularly in the so-called capitalist countries. The money and power resides largely in the huge industrial combines, and compared with industry, there is little if any attempt to apply behavioral science concepts such as the

[1]Chris Argyris, *Intervention Theory and Method* (Reading, Mass.: Addison-Wesley, 1970), p. 136. "An open system is one whose strategy for adaptation is less on building defensive forts and more on reaching out, learning, and becoming competent in controlling the external and internal environment so that its objectives are achieved and its members continue to learn. An open system not only is open to being influenced, but also its members strive to accept every responsibility that helps them increase their confidence in themselves and their group, and increase their capacity to solve problems effectively."

open system.[2] Equally closed are the systems pertaining to law enforcement, particularly the prisons. Most people interested in public affairs, including the prison personnel themselves, subscribe to the belief that in many cases prisons do more harm than good to prisoners and their families; and yet compared with industrial or medical research (good indicators of priorities), relatively little money or interest goes into this social problem.

These are a few of our social problem areas and we want to address ourselves to the role psychiatry plays or should play in reaching the long-term goal of human self-fulfillment. We want to avoid the trap of defining our goal in explicit terms. In my opinion, this is an age of evolution, where many of our traditional concepts are being re-examined and no one value system can hope to gain wide acceptance. The various racial, socioeconomic, and cultural groups are clamoring for attention at this point, and this seems to be equated more with fear or anxiety than with any learning process. But at least previously muted problems are surfacing and *demanding* attention. The almost complete absence of any significant contribution from psychiatry in relation to the social problems of our times such as campus or race riots poses some questions—have we a contribution to make? Do we recognize the motivation in at least some of our members to develop skills in such areas? If so, are we prepared to delegate money, time, and research to develop such problem-solving skills? Already there is much that we can learn from the behavioral sciences in the areas of social system theory, communications theory, and learning theory. But do we want to enter such social problem areas which would mean restructuring

[2]An exception may be made in relation to the Kennedy administration. But the policy to use behavioral scientists and other "experts" did not remain part of future administrations. This suggests that "the country," i.e., the people with power, were not in favor of such an evolution.

our whole postgraduate training and probably undergraduate training too?

It seems that in response to the changing cultural climate and demands of modern living, we are already responding according to our limited skills and particularized goals. Most psychiatrists still cling to the need to identify a consumer as "sick" but are willing to extend their awareness of him from a person with intrapsychic problems to that of a member of a system (family) that may be changeable. Such a systems approach may affect the outcome as much as or more than the application of our traditional psychotherapeutic skills in the doctor/patient relationship. This is the thin edge of the wedge. Many psychiatrists have chosen to leave the security of their office and meet "patients" in their living environment. In the process they have put themselves in a system in which their role has to be redefined, and their power and authority (not to mention their skills) made available to questioning and to influences that are a part of learning and of growth.

One of the basic arguments put forward in this book is the complementarity between teaching and learning. By teaching we often mean the transmission of subject matter from teacher to pupil—a one-way communication process, the object of which is to store (memorize) information. The consumer usually is a passive recipient in this process and may not have any part in the choice of subject matter. Thus, most school children are expected to memorize what "is good for them." The art of teaching includes the skill with which the teacher can obtain the pupil's attention and so initiate the process of retention and memorizing. "Good" students are attentive and can regurgitate information on demand, as in answering examination questions. In such a rigid system, a "bad" student is inattentive and memorizes poorly—he may even question the teacher's choice of subject or "act out" his disinterest in "delinquent" behavior.

This process of one-way communication without interaction is, I think, an inherent part of our culture and in varying degrees permeates the whole field of education, including higher education. But similar trends are discernable in many other fields including the family, industry, religion, and despite the talk about the "democratic" countries, in federal administration too. In all these areas the consumer has relatively little direct control over his relationship with the system or his capacity to change it. Communication is largely one way, from top to bottom in the hierarchy, with the consumer as the passive recipient of decisions made for him by the heads of the organization.

There are signs that this hierarchical authoritarian model is giving way in some areas to a more democratic egalitarian one. Thus, parents are being forced by circumstance to reconsider the nature of their relationships, particularly with their teenage offspring. And there is a growing number of experimental projects in schools and colleges in which the consumer can express his own perception of his needs and operate as a change agent in the system. All to frequently, however, student councils or representation on college boards are token gestures rather than fundamental changes in the direction of an open system. In general, the universities are largely out of touch with the real world where the action is. The same resistance to change is readily demonstrable in industry, where the profit motive and the vested interests of top management contribute to a slow process of dehumanization of employees and consumers.

The same vested interests are apparent in medicine which in many ways is another example of "big business." Hospital costs continue to spiral, doctors' fees rise steadily, and the consumer has little opportunity to contribute to a process of change within the system so that *his* needs can be met. A glaring example of this trend is the steady decline of home visits by the doctor, which are seen as uneconomic.

Yet who would dispute the value of a home visit in the early hours of the morning to an anxious parent whose child is crying and terrified because of an acute otitis media (earache).

By contrast with the above, two-way communication, interpersonal interaction, the sharing of differing viewpoints, and mutual learning can represent part of a process of change within any system. An open system predisposes to learning, and this is why throughout this book one tends to stress its value compared with a closed system. A professor operating within a closed system may add to his knowledge through reading and sharing information with his peers, but his department and his students may feel frustrated by a lack of two-way communication, interpersonal interaction, learning, and growth. Moreover, such a rigid structure precludes for the professor an opportunity for learning within the system. No wonder one talks about the dead hand of academia when heads of departments and teachers shut themselves off from the feedback of valid information from their students and living-learning situations generally.

I frequently use the term social learning.[3] By this I mean two-way communication motivated by some inner need or stress leading to the overt or covert expression of feeling and involving cognitive processes and change. The term implies a change in the individual's attitude and/or beliefs as a result of the experience. These changes are incorporated and modify his personality and self-image.

It is my belief that an open systems approach applied to social units of all kinds, whether in operating theatres, hospitals, community mental health centers, city governments, churches, businesses, prisons, schools, or colleges

[3]Maxwell Jones, *Beyond the Therapeutic Community* (New Haven, Conn.: Yale University Press, 1968), pp. 68–107.

would increase their effectiveness, increase job satisfaction, lower the incidence of illness (both physical and mental), and make the world a happier place. Such a pipe dream is as yet largely lacking in research data, or even in valid information or information science technology. My only justification for such optimism is clinical experience. This has taken me from formal psychiatry at the Maudsley Hospital London, to open systems (therapeutic communities) at Henderson Hospital London, Oregon State Hospital, Salem, Oregon, Dingleton Hospital, Scotland, and Fort Logan Mental Health Center, Denver, Colorado. This momentum has carried me into the school system in Scotland and the United States for the past five years. These experiences have convinced me of the limitations of traditional psychiatry as taught and practiced in closed systems. If psychiatry is to survive and grow as a useful social resource, it has two possible choices: (a) to retrench and develop its specifically psychotherapeutic skills in universities, psychiatric facilities such as state and private hospitals, and private practice; and (b) to follow the trend already favored by many psychiatrists and become involved in community action programs.

It is my belief that the latter course offers most promise for a useful role in society, but what *is* community psychiatry? If we lack valid information to enhance organizational effectiveness in industry where much experience and research is currently developing, we are certainly less prepared in the field of community psychiatry. We have as yet no model of a community mental health program that has achieved anything approaching universal approval. So we must content ourselves with developing a variety of models each aiming at meeting the needs of its particular geographical area. Cultural, racial, and socioeconomic factors, among others, must be considered in both consumer and professional groups. An open system will then allow for two-way communication, shared decision making, and social learning between these two groups. Once such a system is established, it can be studied in terms of its effectiveness.

The role of a leader in such a developing social system is of paramount importance. If he already has a behavioral science approach, as a result of his training (unlikely if he is a psychiatrist) or his experience, he will feel a need to study the social system surrounding the area of the community mental health clinic. He will survey the needs of the population and its various subgroups, by age, economic and work status, and so on. He will try to identify some of the leaders in the community and motivate them to help to develop an effective open system by agreeing to serve on a citizens' board, etc. Only then should a decision be made regarding the type of professional help needed to complement the social action groups already present, or potentially available, in the community.

Part I of this book looks at the social system's approach as it affects society generally and discusses a long-term goal of a society that grows up and is educated in an open system.

Part II is concerned with the evolution of a systems approach to the problems of mental health. The experience of the author in therapeutic communities over the past 25 years gives some, but all too little, valid information in this area.

Part I

SOCIAL SYSTEMS

Chapter 1

THE DYNAMICS OF CHANGE

A system can be thought of as an organized whole unit that includes the interactions of its interdependent component parts and its relationship to the environment.[1] Or, a system is any set of elements related to one another in such a way that changes in one induce changes in one or more of the others.[2,3] The elements of the system are the various jobs that have to be performed as part of the primary task, and the social relations that people must enter into to do these jobs. Together these are referred to as a sociotechnical system. Thus, in times of war, an army is a system

[1]W. Buckley, *Sociology and Modern Systems Theory* (Englewood Cliffs, N.J.: Prentice-Hall, 1967).

[2]A. W. Clark and N. T. Yeomans, 1 (Springer, N.Y.: Fraser House, 1969).

[3]A. D. Hall and R. E. Fagan, "Definition of a System," *Yearbook of the Society for the Advancement of General Systems Theory* 1, (1956), pp. 18–28, define a system as "a set of objects together with relationships between the objects and between their attributes."

supposed to have a common purpose, although recent events in Viet Nam would seem to belie this. Or a hospital has a social organization or system whose goal is to help the sick. There again many individuals who are a part of the system might question if the goal of healing is being met, or is even given first priority by those in charge of the organization. Even more complex is a school system whose purported goal is the education of the young. But what is education? And how can children best be helped to grow up to be effective citizens in the larger systems that constitute society?

We start with the basic assumption that our present-day society has failed in most areas, and indeed, it is hard to find an example of a system that gains overall approval. Obviously different subgroups in society will view the same system from different vantage points, e.g., the "haves" and the "have-nots" in relation to industry, which for most people, is equated with material success and money. But in any one industrial system there is a similar spectrum of attitudes dependent on many variables including pay, status, job satisfaction, career prospects, and so on.

In comparatively recent years a new role and function has appeared on the systems horizon. This has to do with the system's own awareness of itself as a feeling, thinking, functioning entity associated with an overall goal of health and self-fulfillment. This structural and functional self-consciousness is as yet hardly visible, but it is hard to believe that man with his insatiable curiosity, energy, and inventiveness will fail to respond to this new challenge. The open school and the concept of open systems generally is part of this evolutionary process, which was further elaborated in the Forword.

To describe merely the organization of, say, a hospital, presents no particular problems. In modern times it has been assumed that any system will be based on the traditional hierarchical model with the power and prestige identified at the apex of the triangle. Thus, most systems have available an organizational chart which indicates the relative position of each employee in the hierarchy and his job description. A flow chart may also indicate communication, production, and other channels.

What is relatively new is a growing interest in the concept of Organization Development (O.D.).[4,5,6] Sherwood describes this as ". . . an educational process by which human resources are continuously identified, allocated, and expanded in ways that make these resources more available to the organization, and therefore, improve the organization's problem-solving capabilities."

At first sight, such a concept seems to imply interference with the status quo and threatens the security of everyone within the system. The threat is greatest at the upper levels of the hierarchy where power, decision making, controls over behavior, etc. are centralized.

To change the beliefs, attitudes, and values within a system seems presumptuous and questions the traditional concepts of management built up over many decades. The industrial revolution saw the introduction of modern technology, which harnessed the physical forces of manual labor to multiply many times the production of material goods. The people with money and power (the industrialists) benefited enormously, but the employees fared less well, and slowly the state had to intervene to protect the rights of children and employees generally. A balance was later attempted by the development of trade unions to counter the power of the employers and "educate" them in

[4]John J. Sherwood, An Introduction to Organization Development, *The 1972 Annual Handbook for Group Facilitators.* American Psychological Association, Inc., Washington, D.C.

[5]Warren G. Bennis, *Organization Development: Its Nature, Origins, and Prospects* (Reading, Mass.: Addison-Wesley, 1969), p. 2.

[6]Richard Beckhard, *Organization Development* (Reading, Mass.: Addison-Wesley, 1969), p. 9.

understanding of the needs of the employees. In Britain these factors contributed to the growth of an ideology based on the concept of the distribution of wealth and power articulated by the Fabian Society, a group of prominent economists, social scientists, and writers including George Bernard Shaw. The Labour or Socialist Party in Britain set out to practice new political principles that paid heed to the needs of the lower socioeconomic levels of society. But the new beliefs, attitudes, and values propounded by socialism threatened the existing power structure represented by industry, banks, and property owners in general.

These trends were evident in every walk of life in most countries as for example in the school system. The industrial revolution resulted in a need for a labor force that was literate, but passive and conformist. Employees who could "think for themselves" were a threat to the efficiency of an employer-dominated industry. Our present-day school system bears the scars of this conformist era.

The two great world powers, the United States and the Soviet Union, epitomize the polarity that emerged from a world struggling to achieve values compatible with both the new technology and the growing need for a human identity with self-realization.

For long, the American dream of success was identified with the hope of personal achievement fostered by the illusion that equal opportunity existed for everyone. "Go West young man" epitomized this dream and was realized by a sufficient number of self-made millionaires to whet the appetites of the young. But as industry grew more and more successful, it was able to organize into even more powerful combines or corporations. Now the less successful (industrialists) were swallowed up by the more successful, and the question of where the ultimate power in the United States now resides—in the federal government or in industry—is relevant.

It is no mere coincidence that the behavioral sciences in the United States are evolving a new technology for change. The number and excellence of psychologists, sociologists, anthropologists, and other social scientists in the United States far exceeds the resources of all the rest of the world. The developing skills of the behavioral scientists are infiltrating most fields of human endeavor, e.g., schools of business management, industry, new town planning, schools, law enforcement, and so on.

This new approach to systems change (Organization Development or O.D.), unlike most new technologies, tends to keep a low profile. This is not surprising when one considers what such change agents are up against, if they are employees of the system and dependent on the power structure for their jobs. They are not usually overtly identified with O.D. but are in personnel departments or similar familiar designations. They usually have no peer group and feel relatively vulnerable. The absence of colleagues to share problems and learn from heightens their feeling of isolation.

The evolution of this breed of behavioral scientist is primarily the result of a growing interest in the dynamics of human behavior. The psychoanalytic movement is a milestone in this development, but is limited to intrapsychic exploration of one individual by his analyst. Slowly more attention has been given to the environmental forces influencing behavior, and groups for training and treatment have grown rapidly. The National Training Laboratory, associated with Bethel, Maine, gives a formal identity to this movement and sensitivity training courses are made available to interested laymen, many from the fields of industry and mental health.[7] This is important because al-

[7] I am using the term "sensitivity training" in relation to group dynamics rather than management and in relation to group goals rather than individual treatment.

though the big bosses in industry seldom go to such courses, they allow their junior executives to go, and so the basic concepts of two-way communication, shared decision making, and learning as a social process are infiltrating into the business system.

Psychiatry too is playing its part in this evolution. Group treatment, a derivitive of psychoanalysis, is becoming more involved with the real world of the patient primarily through family treatment groups and marriage counseling groups. More recently, home visits have developed along with crisis intervention in the family system and attempts to relocate mental health personnel in community mental health clinics near the communities in which the clients live. The consumer is being given a new identity. He is becoming a significant partner in a change system aimed at bettering his own and his family's adjustment to life.

Systems theory and O.D. had their early advocates in psychiatry long before O.D. had emerged in any identifiable form a decade ago. The therapeutic community was conceptualized a quarter of a century ago and was an early model for change. It will be discussed at length in Part II.

The Goals of Organization Development

The definition of O.D. used by Bennis includes the statement that it is "a complex educational strategy intended to change the beliefs, attitudes, values, and structure of organizations."[8] He admits freely that O.D. is in its infancy, "yet it holds promise for developing the 'real knowledge' about our post-modern world."[9] While much knowledge exists about the basic nature of social organizations, relatively little is known about how to *change* these

[8]Bennis, *Organization Development,* p. 2.
[9]Ibid., p. 2.

systems. Peter Vaill, talking about the experiences of O.D. practitioners, says, "There was a consistent expression among them of knowing *what* they wanted to do but having to rely on intuition and on-the-spot invention of techniques for accomplishing it."[10] What the practitioners wanted was to achieve an atmosphere of mutual trust and respect in the working relationships within the system. But these norms were at variance with those of the system, particularly with those at the top. As yet, however, there is no definite proof that the norms of O.D., which include open communication, shared decision making, and learning as a social process, are necessarily valid and if applied will enhance the effectiveness of a system. There is a lack of research evidence in this direction. However, there are models of systems change which at this point can only be studied descriptively. Summerhill, the experimental school developed by A. S. Neill, is an early model described eloquently in Neill's book.[11] The impact of this experiment is hard to assess, but the system was certainly the forerunner of much of the current interest in "open" or "free" schools.[12] The first book on therapeutic communities served a similar purpose.[13] The richest field for descriptive accounts of organization development have been written by consultants in industry. Argyris gives an extensive bibliography in this field.[14] These descriptive accounts have helped to develop the tentative theories of O.D. These are then available for

[10]Peter B. Vaill, *The Practice of Organization Development* (Madison, Wis.: American Society for Training and Development, 1970).

[11]A. S. Neill, *Summerhill: A Radical Approach to Child Rearing* (New York: Hart Publishers, 1960).

[12]Charles E. Silberman, *Crisis in the Classroom* (New York: Random House, Vintage Books, 1970).

[13]Maxwell Jones, *The Therapeutic Community* (New York: Basic Books, 1953).

[14]Argyris, *Intervention Theory and Method* (Reading, Mass.: Addison-Wesley, 1970).

more exact research and the eventual establishment of a methodology.

In view of the above statements, it would appear that we are not yet in a position to formulate the goals of O.D. with any precision or conviction. But much the same arguments could be raised in connection with business management, psychoanalysis, or education in general.

Perhaps the best attempt to outline the goals of O.D. is that of Beckhard.[15] He defines O.D. as "an effort (1) planned (2) organization-wide and (3) managed from the top, to (4) increase organization effectiveness and health through (5) planned interventions in the organization's 'processes' using behavioral-science knowledge."[16]

The whole question of O.D. in relationship to its present-day standing and practices is discussed in relationship to the clinical skills, training, and competence of O.D. consultants.[17] They refute the argument that much of O.D. practice seems to hinge on sensitivity training or T-Group confrontation.[18] Such training groups have as their primary goal learning about the self in a small-group context. This is a much narrower concept than Beckhard's outline of the goals of O.D.[19]

What is a valid framework from which to grow? Argyris states that "one way to accelerate the processes of building a framework is to borrow from the frameworks of other fields where more systematic empirical research is available. For example, intervention activity is carried on by

[15]Richard Beckhard, *Organization Development* (Reading, Mass.: Addison-Wesley, 1969), pp. 9–19.

[16]Ibid., p. 9.

[17]Burke W. Warner, Harry Levinson, and Harry Sashkin, "Organization Development Pro and Con," *Professional Psychology* 4 (May 1973): 187–200.

[18]L. P. Bradford, J. R. Gibb, and K. D. Benne, *T-Group Theory and Laboratory Method* (New York: John Wiley & Sons, 1964).

[19]Beckhard, *Organization Development,* pp. 9–19.

individuals or groups with individuals, groups, intergroups, and organizations as clients. Consequently, the research in interpersonal relations, group dynamics, intergroup relations, and organizational behavior may help to provide the beginnings of an early foundation."[20]

One of the most powerful factors in any change system is the reaction against personal hurt. The motivation for much O.D. comes from individuals who feel that their personal growth is being stifled and their creative potential ignored. Thus, the people in an industrial organization most likely to conceive of the possibility of change are the junior executives who have extensive education in the traditional college sense and may have participated in sensitivity training groups, read extensively, etc. Such executives also know their own subsystem better than the director, although they may concede his wider perspective in relation to the total organization. But they can better bridge the gap between workers and employers and are often ready to formulate plans for a totally new social structure. Hence, it is not surprising that most of the "movement" toward system change comes from this level of the hierarchy.

Much the same factors apply in the hospital system and particularly in the field of psychiatry. Experience in group work training, psychodynamics, family therapy, etc., has changed the perspective and values of many psychiatrists. No longer content with the limitations of the doctor-patient relationship, psychiatrists are becoming much more sensitive to the social environment and the vision of social system change as an effective therapeutic agent. So there are good reasons for such a systems approach to be studied and developed in the field of mental health.

In every system there is room for improvement and change. Different individuals will perceive the need in

[20]Argyris, *Intervention Theory and Method,* p. 14.

different ways and this may lead to a stalemate. Thus, a family may learn to live with the frustration of a parent who will not listen, while the parent sees the same situation as disobedience in the children. Or a sales department in a firm may have poor morale because the staff feels it has no emotional investment in the firm, while the manager complains of lack of efficiency and interest from the staff.

Is there a methodology to effect change, comparable to, say the marriage counselor, group therapist, or psychoanalyst?[21] Counseling or treatment presuppose an individual or small group of individuals who are conscious of a need for help and believe there is a socially acceptable method of obtaining help. This argument applies in part to our middle class culture, but hardly at all to the lower socioeconomic levels of our society. Even middle class people find it hard to seek out professional help. The fear is that to become a patient may carry a social stigma. There is also the feeling of failure and the loss of self-esteem in not successfully managing one's own affairs. Nevertheless, the anxiety and emotional hurt may provide the motivation to take the plunge and seek professional help. This well-worn pathway has as yet no equivalent in social systems in general. The child or teenager has little or no awareness of the possibility of change; nor has the average parent, or school teacher. Social problems have to reach crisis proportions or be identified as "sickness" before professional help is sought.

We will return to this theme over and over again—why do the helping services have to sit on the sidelines, waiting for problem situations to blow up before they can legitimately become involved? Or put another way, why can't the helping professions become involved in any system in trou-

[21]Jack Rotham, *Three Models of Community Organization Practice,* from National Conference on Social Welfare, Social Work Practice 1965 (New York: Columbia University Press, 1968).

ble, so that people can be helped to help themselves before a crisis occurs? In other words, why can't they become proactive (influencing the environment) rather than reactive at a later stage of crisis.

Carrying this point of view to its logical conclusion, we know that every system is frequently "at risk" and education in terms of systems theory should start before birth so it can be a significant part of child rearing and family relationships. This study of group behavior and the dynamics of interaction would then bridge the interface between home and school. Education for human relations and problem solving has hardly begun in the home and school systems. The end result of traditional education based on memorizing subject matter and passing exams with its norms of conformity, competition, and lack of compassion highlights the need for an applied systems theory and change.

The helping professions were originally modeled on the doctor-patient relationship. No one, we assume, wants to die. The doctor gets much of his status, prestige, and financial reward from this basic fact. The ideal of the family doctor, skilled technician, friend, and confidant lingers on even though it now has little validity in fact (in the United States). The Hippocratic oath implies that the profession still believes in its dedication to the needs of the patient and to confidentiality, even though changing circumstances seem to call for a different code of ethics. To give two bipolar examples: to do our "best" for patients in hospitals would call for patient-centered rather than staff-centered hospital systems, but to include the family in open communication with the patient's problem may be a negative use of the doctor's authority and the concept of confidentiality.

One further point, doctors and the helping professions generally tend to operate in a one-to-one relationship with an identified patient. There is a beginning trend in social psychiatry to operate with the family system and even some subsection of the community surrounding the problem area, but always under the banner of mental health.

Once we leave the positive aura of medicine, the problems of credibility begin. What system welcomes an outsider probing their intimate or factual problems? What group would not ask themselves questions like the following? How can an outsider be trusted and what evidence have we of his competence to effect the changes we feel are necessary? After all, he does not know us and may only see us through the eyes of the department head who engaged him. Is he going to manipulate us into an even more subservient relationship with the boss? We are told to talk openly in the group of our peers so that we can identify our problems and this "outsider" will help us to bring about change; but do I risk losing my job if I speak out?

Since the turn of the century, industry has employed outside consultants to effect change. But these sponsors of scientific management, e.g. Frederik Taylor and Max Weber, were efficiency experts dealing with material facts such as time and motion studies. Their influence is still strong, but whatever benefits industry has derived from their efforts, there is a growing awareness that they have contributed to the dehumanization of the workers' world. Charlie Chaplin paid eloquent tribute to this problem in his film *Modern Times.* That this lack of concern for the worker as an individual is creating serious problems in morale, with frustration leading to alcohol and drug abuse, broken marriages, mental health problems, etc., is documented in a recent report issued by H.E.W.[22]

Against this background, the organization development movement (O.D.) has grown up during the past decade. It is no mere chance that this organization is domi-

[22]U.S. Department of Health, Education and Welfare, *Work in America* (Cambridge, Mass.: The M.I.T. Press, 1972).

nated by social psychologists and other behavioral scientists interested in the action field. The leaders are all associated with the National Training Laboratory (N.T.L.) movement and an extensive knowledge and interest in group dynamics is part of their basic training. The opportunity to become interested in large systems, as opposed to small groups, was afforded by industry. Scientific management consultants did not seem to provide the answer to the growing discontent among workers. Absenteeism and turnover rates were rising while in many instances morale was falling.

Managers were faced by a realization that the world was changing at an ever-increasing rate and the younger generation was no longer prepared to accept the conformist values and the authority system that typified the post-industrial revolution era. How does one keep pace with the challenges of a technological age plus the changes in social values? The more socially conscious and open-minded managers began to look for help in the area of human relations and social organization. They were prepared to pay consultants to help them through this process of change. How does a relatively static system, whether in medicine, education, industry, or any other sphere gain momentum in the direction of openness to change?

We will identify three phases: (1) a preliminary or team-building phase, (2) a process or action phase, and (3) an evaluative or evolutionary phase.

Chapter 2

PRELIMINARY OR TEAM-BUILDING PHASE

Two-Way Communication (Words and Feelings)

In ordinary conversation we monitor what we say and how we say it. We choose our words to fit the situation as we see it. We try to make a good impression by saying the right things and by trying to communicate appropriate feelings. Only in the security of our innermost circle of friends do we drop this façade and show our "true" selves through what we say and how we say it. This goal of open communication is hard to achieve and depends partly on two elusive factors: trust and training. I say elusive because we ourselves are often uncertain of the extent to which we trust our social and work contacts and our attitudes toward people are constantly changing with changing circumstances. Training, too, can be an elusive factor if it implies change in attitudes and beliefs. To take a course of lectures on communication may increase one's knowledge of the subject, but does nothing to modify the defensive façade that is so characteristic of ordinary conversation.

To promote open communication depends on many factors which we will examine later. Our first concern is to establish a climate that enhances the communication process. Thus, a friendly atmosphere in a familiar environment is a start. The expectations regarding open communication must be radically different if we meet in the boss's office, or in the staff lounge. The purpose of open communication must have meaning for everyone attending the meeting and preferably the people attending have come of their own volition and are motivated both to participate and to listen. Seats arranged in a circle make everyone present both visible and physically equal—no one is at the head of the table.

But a favorable climate and motivation are not enough. The group may be too big, e.g., a board of directors or a class of 20 to 30 people may feel a loss of identity and be overawed by the weight of numbers. The number eight to ten, dear to the hearts of group psychotherapists, may materially aid open communication. Here the factor of personal familiarity may play a big part. A team of 20 to 30 individuals whose work or play brings them into daily contact with each other may feel more comfortable and interested collectively than if broken up into two or three smaller groups.

The biggest factor, however, is training. It is as though in our culture we have to be trained not to be "honest." For most of us, neither at home nor at school were our true feelings or opinions sought. There were definite rules regulating communication, ranging from the dictum "children should be seen and not heard" to the strictures imposed by having to be "polite," to the crushing adult admonishment of "you kids just don't understand." To seek to bypass all these patterns of a lifetime and have open communication is an unreasonable expectation.

The group must share common interests and goals and have a strong motivation to change before it can risk testing direct expression of thoughts and feelings. In a mental health setting, this process with a group of patients is called treatment. In a group of mental health workers, students, etc., the process is called training.[1] In either case it is a relatively new experience and it takes many weeks or months to overcome the fear of being misunderstood, misjudged, disliked, ostracized, punished, victimized, etc., all of which fears help determine our original defenses and personality façade.

To take such a risk may seem unjustified to the family man who sees it as jeopardizing his social or job security. The risks must be matched against the prospective gains. If these gains fail to materialize, the motivation to change will disappear.

Thus, learning to communicate in an open system is a big undertaking, carrying with it no guarantee of a success-

[1]I realize that it is usual to equate treatment with symptoms and mental pathology. The therapist uncovers the pathological thinking and makes it available to the patient who can then see his conflict (often unconscious before treatment) in a more balanced perspective. This "adjustment" is accompanied by the relief of symptoms which according to Freud are substitutes for missing satisfactions.

Training, on the other hand, has an educational orientation with a view to increasing knowledge and skills. It does not intentionally focus on mental pathology. But in the field of human behavior, it is often impossible to say where deviancy ends and pathology begins. Taking a school classroom as one example, a teacher may try to understand an emotional disturbance in a group of her pupils. Given the necessary interest and skill, she may help her pupils to understand something of the dynamics of their emotional problem. In this case the symptoms can be equated with frustration leading to deviant behavior. Understanding of the dynamics of this behavior may substitute more appropriate behavior (and satisfaction) for the acting out behavior.

My contention is that treatment and training both have similar goals, i.e., social learning and social maturation, and in this context may be used synonymously.

ful outcome and even a danger of disaster. And yet without open communication and involvement, learning (growing) as a social process is virtually impossible. We will return to the subject of social learning later.

Relevant Information Exchange

The what, why, and how of communication is clearly relevant to any information gathering. The information must in some way be relevant to both individual and group needs. It is this sharing of information that contributes to a group identity. Individuals become aware of their common identity with others through shared needs and tentative goals. At the same time, goals must not be imposed by the majority, and free choice of areas of interest must be retained at this early stage of group interaction.

An example of a meeting geared to learning might help in understanding this concept. The setting was a state hospital ward meeting, with approximately twenty patients and ten staff members from various mental health disciplines. This particular ward had a relatively open system, and the patients shared with the staff the responsibility for problem solving, setting limits on behavior, examining social values, etc. The staff had a democratic, egalitarian structure with a relatively flat hierarchy and shared leadership and decision making. A patient acted as chairman for the meeting and the first agenda item came from the patients. They had invited a nurse, Sandra, to stay on after night duty to attend the meeting and she had agreed. Three female patients all communicated a negative image of this nurse—she never smiled, was irritable when approached at nights by the patients needing help, and was "stuck-up."

Sandra remained calm and reminded the chairman that on his arrival in hospital, he had commented on her serious demeanor, and she had replied, "You do not have to smile in order to be happy." The input of information varied from positive comments on her efficiency, strength, and skill in handling crisis situations to criticism that partly supported the original accusations. Sandra answered some questions about herself as a person—no, she was not married and she lived alone with her dog. She liked her work as a nurse but at times found it difficult to reconcile the patients' demands with what was considered "good" treatment. This applied particularly to sedatives for some patients (including one of the original complainants) who had asked for such help before they even tried to get to sleep.

The staff avoided becoming defensive by remaining relatively objective and interacting freely with the patients. Another nurse asked if the problem really centered on Sandra, and she implied that the patients were overdependent on the staff.

The patients responded indicating their need for support and love. Did the staff really care about the patients or was it simply a job to them? They admitted that this insecurity reached its height at nighttime when there were only two staff members on duty.

Sandra was able to say that she was glad that she had responded to the patients' request to attend the meeting on her off-duty time, and the meeting had greatly reduced her anxiety. The tension had gone out of the meeting, and both patients and staff seemed to have a feeling of positive identification with the ward system.

These meetings occurred daily and demonstrated the value of relevant information exchange.

Frequent Group Interaction (Meetings)

To build up an open communication system and valid information exchange requires regularly scheduled meetings of the same individuals. This opportunity for interaction between individuals forms the basis for the future process of change through social learning and growth. We seem to have built-in defenses against meetings. One good reason is that for most of us they conjure up an image of a captive audience listening to some teacher or authority speaking to and not with the group. The idea of interaction for the purpose of listening to various points of view so that one's awareness of new dimensions may be heightened is relatively unfamiliar. The familiar pattern in all education is the lesson or lecture. The subject matter is known to the teacher whose job it is to impart this knowledge to the pupil. Teaching in this sense is clearly important, but should not exclude the other dimension of education which is learning through interaction and an analysis of the feelings engendered. We will return to learning as an interactional process when considering the concept of social learning.

To be viable a system must be in touch with its environment. Relevant information input can be seen as a source of energy for the system. What happens to the input as it passes through the system is called the throughput.[2] The working through of the input by the system inevitably modifies it. This is one of the basic principles of an open system. Input of relevant information leads to interaction and initiates the process of social learning. Even without this learning process, the information output must have value to the environment. At Henderson Hospital near London, the information input of supposed police brutality shared by patients and staff at a community meeting might result in a greater awareness by the patients of the difficulties experienced by law enforcement officers and the outcome might be a better relationship between patients,

[2]D. Katz and R. L. Kahn, *The Social Psychology of Organizations* (New York, John Wiley & Sons, 1966).

many of whom had at one time been apprehended by the police, and the police force itself. A negative outcome with retaliatory violence did at times endanger the survival of the system.

The concept of throughput is a valuable one for change systems. Too often a system tends to pay insufficient attention to its external environment, behaving as though it existed in a vacuum. Unless its value to the environment is demonstrated constantly, inputs will be curtailed and the future of the system may be jeopardized. This danger to the system will be communicated in the form of feedback which is an integral part of two-way communication. Feedback of a positive kind reinforces "good" behavior and is the basis of all forms of behavior modification. While medical superintendent of Dingleton Hospital, Scotland, I kept in close touch with the surrounding community including the power system (employers) in Edinburgh. My feedback to the hospital system from the outside environment helped to maintain a dynamic sequence of input, throughput, output-feedback, and further input.

Trust

During the preliminary phase of team building one of the greatest difficulties is the development of trust along the team members. Trust can only evolve through time. The degree of trust will be related to the performance of the group and of the leader or leaders. Times of crisis test the motivation, skill, and integrity of the group. Failure to resolve problems at such times may undermine confidence and halt the process of growth and the individual or group's willingness to take risks. The strength of the group identity is largely dependent on the overall level of trust. If splinter groups emerge, based on many possible factors including distrust of other subgroups, then communication will be limited and much of the group's energy will be wasted on internal disputes and misunderstandings. Trust is an essential prerequisite of social learning and growth.

Trust is a very complex concept meaning different things to different people. We have touched on some of its more familiar (and superficial) attributes. At a deeper (feeling) level trust involves an intimate sharing of feelings and social learning. In this context it will take many months of constant group interaction, at a feeling as well as at a cognitive level, for a group of individuals to accomplish this level of trust with each other. Even so, events will constantly test this degree of trust and much will depend on the skill and integrity of the leader or leaders to turn crisis into learning situations that may enhance rather than destroy the degree of trust. Practical considerations may prevent such a process of growth and trust. The rapid turnover of staff so frequent in this technological age, the repetitive cycle of trainees, e.g., psychiatric residents who spend from three to twelve months in any one treatment setting, the resistance to change (sharing of feelings, etc.) so characteristic of senior officials with power and control, are among many factors that preclude any deep level of trust in certain situations.

This may pose one of the more serious dilemmas of our time. In an age in which we are faced with the splitting of social units into more and more temporary and competing subcultures, how can we hope to achieve any deep degree of trust. To cite one example: social mobility, so characteristic of the American scene, demands an unprecedented capacity to form short-term social relationships and repeat this process time after time. Can children meet this challenge when faced by frequent change of school, new companions, and differing cultures? Toffler expounds on this theme and the increasing rate of social change which will tax to the limit our capacity to adapt and to find self-fulfillment.[3]

[3]Alvin Toffler, *Future Shock* (New York: Random House, 1970).

Leadership

It is an oversimplification to think that an open system creates its leaders in response to circumstance, and that the individual best qualified to lead in a particular situation will automatically emerge within the group. I have written extensively on multiple leadership in a multidisciplinary setting.[4,5] To quote Ken Morrice, "It is a paradox worth recognizing that a democracy to be efficient needs good leadership. And a further paradox is suggested: that democracy can be maintained only from a position of power."[6]

Every social system tends to evolve its own authority structure from the traditional autocratic hierarchical structure at one extreme to the democratic egalitarian model at the other. If we think of a system in its purposive aspects, it is evident that at least one person is already committed to achieve that purpose. Usually that person is seen as the logical leader, at least during the initial stages of the project. He is essential as the creator and initial sponsor and the extent of internal commitment by the others will depend, in part, on his capacity to communicate his ideas, the relevance of his information, the trust he engenders throughout the system, and his own performance under stress. In this context the leader comes to be seen as the person best suited to give direction to the group so that its goal or goals can constantly be kept in mind. His function is not necessarily equated with power or authority. As the initiator of the project, he may, and usually does, have this potential power, but may choose to delegate this aspect of his function to those individuals whose functions require power and authority for effective implementation.

[4]Jones, *Beyond the Therapeutic Community.*

[5]Maxwell Jones, *Social Psychiatry in Practice* (Middlesex, England: Penguin Books, 1968.)

[6]J. K. W. Morrice, "Myth and the Democratic Process," *British Journal of Medical Psychology* 45 (1972): 327–331.

We are developing a model that will, we hope, facilitate change. One aspect of such a model is the distribution of power and authority throughout the system to reinforce role potential. In this way the chief change agent, the originator of the plan, is freed from many responsibilities that are shared by the system as a whole and is able to give his undivided attention to facilitating the process of change. We have coined the term facilitator for this role. Such an individual is rare, and the originator like the owner-director of a firm usually wants to retain control of his organization and have the final decision-making power.

I have outlined some of the factors that we see as important in the preliminary phase of team building which are the prerequisites of a system for change. Given these factors, how do we conceptualize the process of change?

Chapter 3

THE PROCESS PHASE (ACTION PHASE)

Facilitator or Interventionist

We have already touched on the system whose existence reflects the visionary goals of its creator. Thus, an experimental school might be funded by research money to explore new methods of learning; how to examine social values or understand behavior and problem solving would need a master plan. Such a plan is usually under the direction of the creator or creators of the plan. Such creative individuals seldom get the free hand and opportunity they deserve. Even with such sanctions, the colleagues they recruit, no matter how positively motivated, will have the inevitable "growing pains" before they become a team as described in the preliminary phase.

Much more typically, the system has evolved on bureaucratic lines, with directors who come and go, and the power in the hands of one authority figure or board of directors. The goals of the system apart from such generalizations as "to make money" or "to educate the young" are not clearly formulated at the top, and certainly are of no concern (officially) to the system as a whole. There is no natural leader, as in the previous example where the system grew around one creative change agent. Under these circumstances the system may not have the capacity to initiate change or identify the factors contributing to stagnation, poor morale, or absence of job satisfaction, etc. Lacking a leader within its own ranks (other than the power that controls), the system may turn to some outside consultant for help in identifying their own problems or symptoms and defining their long-term goals. Chris Argyris uses the term interventionist for such a person. He states, "To intervene is to enter into an ongoing system of relationship, to come between or among persons, groups, or objects for the purpose of helping them. There is an important implicit assumption in the definition that should be made explicit: the system exists independently of the intervenor."[1] I would like to make a distinction between a facilitator as a change agent operating from *within* the system, and an interventionist who comes as a consultant from *outside* the system and has a time-limited function. The latter is essentially a trainer helping the personnel to learn new skills so that they can develop and maintain an open system and eventually operate without his help, i.e., he has a specific training function and a specific goal.

The interventionist may, through time, become indistinguishable from the facilitator, i.e., his role may become a permanent one operating from within the system. This presupposes that more and more people in leadership positions will have as part of their basic training an exposure to the theories of communication, learning, organization development, group dynamics, management theory, and so on. Admittedly none of these theories can claim to be "sci-

[1]Argyris, *Intervention Theory and Method,* p. 15.

entific" and at this point in time are largely descriptive hypotheses, and validation is on a trial and error basis. In view of these uncertainties it is useful to think of a facilitator as a change agent operating from within the system but not limited to an open system goal.

At a time when the field is wide open to testing new theories and building new models to study, the facilitator as inspirational leader has considerable value. The early models for change in the school system had such leadership —Maria Montessori[2] and A. S. Neill[3] both in their own way were facilitators and creative leaders in imaginative school systems. These early models of a system for change could be studied at first hand, and certainly contributed to a growing awareness of the limitations of traditional education as little more than "knowledge factories" producing standardized products. The practices and philosophies of such pioneers lent themselves to further research in an attempt to validate the theories propounded. Susan Isaacs, a psychoanalyst, Jerome Bruner, an educational psychologist, and Jean Piaget, the Swiss biologist-psychologist fall into this category.[4,5,6] At the other end of the spectrum are thinkers like Ivan Illich, who do not operate as facilitators in an ongoing system, but question the need for a school system at all—or at least of the kind that has evolved in our culture. "Schooling (as opposed to education) has become our modern dogma, a sacred cow which all must worship, serve, and submit to, yet from which little true

[2]Maria Montessori, *The Child in the Family,* trans. Nancy Cirillo (Chicago: Chicago Registery, 1970).

[3]Neill, *Summerhill.*

[4]Susan Isaacs, *The Children We Teach* (London: University of London Press, 1932).

[5]Jerome Bruner, *Toward a Theory of Instruction* (Cambridge, Mass.: Harvard University Press, Belknap Press, 1966).

[6]Jean Piaget and Barbel Inhelder, *The Psychology of the Child* (New York: Basic Books, 1969).

nourishment is derived."[7] Illich calls for a cultural revolution in education, freeing schools from their present mandatory attendance, the formation of skill centers to replace formal lessons, and peer-matching where the experts can share their knowledge with those seeking instruction.

We are giving the facilitator a far less structured role than the interventionist. He is an evolutionist not as yet limited by the strictures of a systematized theory (organization development). In fact, such systematization may be a trap to be avoided during this early "creative" phase. Conceptualization, systems theory, and organic research may come later if the creative leader is to share his ideas with others and demonstrate his ideas in action by playing the role of facilitator.

The facilitator can be proactive (influencing the environment) provided his input is congruent with the stated goal of the organization. Thus, if the theme under discussion is open communication, the facilitator might confront some of the participants with their behavior and suggest that they have been using their power to block communication at the lower levels of the hierarchy. Such an interpretation, if accurate, frees communication and draws attention to other feeling levels of interaction that may be covert. The point is that the facilitator helps the process of change but does not direct it.

However, the distinction between facilitator and interventionist becomes very arbitrary, as for instance when a facilitator, in order to further the shared goal of open communication, helps the system to see the need to establish regular meetings at all levels of the organization to discuss problems of communication. He might help the system to realize its basic need for a closed as opposed to an open system thus facilitating change in the direction that the majority of individuals in the system wanted to go.

[7]Ivan Illich, *Deschooling Society* (New York: Harper and Row, 1970).

The interventionist, on the other hand, has already been trained in systems theory and may see his role as an educator, and in this sense, his inputs have a predetermined goal of O.D. theory. Argyris himself, the creator of the term, warns repeatedly against confusing theory with fact. His book, *Intervention Theory and Method,* carefully avoids overstatement or dogma. Nevertheless, with all our limitations of knowledge and proof in this field of organization development, it does offer an evolving methodology for change agents. We hope that the "openness" of the intervention approach will not lose its flexibility and drift toward dogma, as evidenced in part by education, medicine, and other systems.

At the present stage of evolution, we are left in a dilemma regarding the "freedom" accorded the roles of facilitator (working from within the system, of which he may have been the creator) and the interventionist (introduced temporarily in the system armed with a methodology for effecting change). The tendency in education is for future leaders in the various professions to be trained in increasingly "open" and less traditional methods. Thus, the lecture, a form of one-way communication of subject matter to be memorized, is giving way slowly to a more open form of two-way communication, interaction, and learning as a social process. The professor in such a system no longer professes to know all the answers, and dogma or speculation can be separated from known facts. In the process, the professor may learn as much, or more, than his students; or at least he may be stimulated to further inquiry or research.

If we anticipate a time when, say the training of a future school principal will include much of what we now call systems theory, will a new dogma tend to emerge? The very concept of an open system (defined on page xiv, footnote 1), aims to avoid such a danger, but as yet we have no proof that such will be the case. In this context the success of the "open" school in the United States, based on the model of the new English Primary Schools is highly controversial.[8] The traditional school, with its rigid rules, teaching as opposed to learning, lack of interaction or responsible roles for pupils is replaced by a more pupil-centered system with emphasis on spontaneity, free choice, and shared responsibility. Each extreme has its ardent supporters, but the evidence to date suggests that on the basis of evaluative tests some children do better in one type of school and some in the other.[9]

One danger would appear to be the tendency to think of "traditional" in negative terms, and "liberal" in positive and progressive, thus better terms.

In brief, by retaining the word facilitator to describe a role in which a catalytic function is fulfilled, one hopes to foster the concept of an evolutionary process. The danger is that such a facilitator may use the system for his own ends, and the group, instead of sharing in the process of change, is manipulated toward a predetermined goal. I experienced such a dilemma in building a hospital system, playing the role of facilitator over a period of 12 years at Henderson Hospital near London. A growing awareness of the dangers of manipulation led to the growth of group responsibility, and in particular, the emergence of alternate leaders who responded to manipulation by confrontation, interaction, and social learning within the administrative group. This phenomenon will be discussed further in Part II when considering the concept of a therapeutic community in a hospital. Of interest here is the fact that what emerged was an open system, basically similar to the model put forward by the behavioral scientists. The fact that this model for change antedated organization development or

[8]Silberman, *Crisis in the Classroom.*

[9]Nicolaus Mills, "Free Versus Directed Schools," *I.R.C.D. Bulletin* 7, 4 September 1971.

systems theory by more than a decade is not surprising. The same could be said of other early models of change systems. They merely tend to confirm or validate the systems approach in that similar principles have evolved independently of the current theory of organization development.

In discussing social systems, the tendency is to think of the facilitator as an entity or an abstraction in much the same way as the term physician or doctor implies certain skills of a definitive kind. The relationship between skills and personality is well recognized and the complementarity of these two factors may largely determine outcome, whether positive or negative.

Less commonly recognized is the importance of the system of relationships surrounding the person of the facilitator. His own self-image and group identity will inevitably be influenced by the people he relates to in the work situation. Clearly, another constellation of relationships affects his self-image in his private life, but this is not our concern here.

In the traditional hierarchal model, the leader has the power that allows him to choose his subordinates and alter their composition at will. Thus, an insecure or autocratic leader surrounds himself with people whom he can "trust" to support his viewpoint and so reinforce his own self-image as a leader, e.g., he may see himself as an imaginative administrator, a "good guy" liked by his subordinates, and so on. He may even believe that he is a "democratic" leader, listening to and being influenced by his colleagues. Such a leader, whether a director in a business, a college professor, a shop steward, or a parent, will exclude himself from the process of learning and personal growth. The effect on the subordinates, workmen, students, children, etc., is equally negative.

At the other extreme, and much less commonly, the leader may choose colleagues not only for their qualifications, skills, and aptitudes for a particular job, but also because they have the strength of personality to stand up to him. Such colleagues by their reaction to the leader at whatever level of communication, alert him to the way his performance is perceived in his immediate social system. In this way, the leader's image of himself is constantly modified and the process of learning is enhanced. With such a model at the top, everyone in the social system may expect a similar increased self-awareness from the social environment at work.

The possibility of an enhanced self-awareness and resulting increase of feedback at all levels from the social environment lead to a phenomenon that we might call containment. Thus, a highly competent and aggressive leader may be protected from his negative potential by this process of containment. His creativity or drive is not part of an ego trip, but is contained within the system to the benefit of the group as a whole. A new idea or insight, even if it emanates from the person of the leader, is shared by the group, and inevitably modified by the process of interaction and so becomes, at least in part, a group idea. An urgent need to take action by the leader can be contained by the group until it has been processed and incorporated by the group and a shared plan of action is evolved.

This concept of containment implies a willingness on the part of the leader to delegate responsibility and power to the group. It also implies a willingness to share his inspirations, ideas, and need fulfillment with the group. This transition is at the heart of our concept of a facilitator, i.e., a leader within a system who shares or delegates power and responsibility to his colleagues so that he is freed from much of his formal administrative (power) role, in order to direct his skills in the direction of an organization compatible with the group needs.

In brief, containment adds a dimension to the facilitator-group interrelationship whereby the positive attributes of the facilitator (leader) are shared by the group, while the negative attributes are canceled out or contained.

At the other end of the spectrum is the concept of hatching. We all know leaders who are inarticulate or hold back inputs for various personality reasons. The staff and patients or consumers may realize such an individual's potential and make conscious efforts to increase his communication skills. In this way the system is benefited by his experience and skills by a process that has a supportive element, which contrasts sharply with the concept of containment. It has been said that a group gets the leadership it deserves; in other words, an open system may help to modify and sharpen the effectiveness of its leader's performance.

The interventionist armed with a methodology for which he has been trained, has, compared with the facilitator, a more specific function to serve during his temporary stay within the system that engages his services. Theoretically, he is there to realize the potential for growth already within the system and tries not to respond to his own preferences, prejudices, or needs. In the process, he may enhance the function of a charismatic leader or facilitator already present in the system. But this must not be at the expense of the group's need fulfillment. His objective and temporary role gives him an opportunity to use conflict, misunderstanding, rivalry, etc., to create social learning. He is hopefully not identified with any faction and can listen to both sides of an argument and in turn be listened to. Thus, he is in an ideal position to further the process of learning. He may help the group to fully utilize the creative ideas of the facilitator in their midst without jeopardizing their group identity and without their being subject to manipulation.

We have reached a point where we can say that many systems have natural leaders who may have an inherent sensitivity that prevents them from abusing their authority and leads to a group identity in which each member can develop his own potential but in relation to the group needs as a whole. It might be argued that a charismatic leader, who is also a facilitator, might be hindered rather than helped if an outside consultant were engaged. No matter how skillful such a consultant's approach, he would inevitably effect the system and reflect some of his ideas and methodology through his interaction with the team. The goal of an open system is, in the present state of our knowledge, highly desirable. But even this goal will be interpreted differently by each system, depending on the training, skills, motivation, and personalities of its individual members, and the function the system serves (health, education, industry, etc.).

I feel that the danger of an outsider "contaminating" the field should not be ignored. In addition, a charismatic leader who is also a natural facilitator may do better without outside help from an interventionist, and this affords an interesting control model of a change system. Finally, in the absence of firm proof of the value of systems theory, other models of apparently successful organization development may throw up many challenging ideas and comparisons. In this contrast, changing circumstances may call for changes in social organization.

At times of crisis, every system tends to clear and simplify its communication channels in preparation for instant action. Failure to do this may lead to disaster. It would be folly to call a meeting to discuss action when the building is on fire. A direct line of authority spells efficiency in such circumstances. But what constitutes a crisis and under what circumstances is a democratic decision-making process to be preferred?

An open system may be developed in an industry with gratifying early results attributable apparently to greater sharing of power, responsibility, and decision making throughout the system, but a crisis may call for another social organization. In one example of participative management, a small electronics firm employing over 200 workers and several part-time management consultants increased its sales 30 per cent between the years 1960 and 1965, workers increased their skills, the job of quality control inspector was dropped, and customer complaints on product quality dropped by 70 per cent.[10] Following the crisis in the aerospace industry (the firm's chief customers), orders dropped by 50 per cent, and the management was forced to cut the workforce in half. The president and owner of the firm now took over control himself and expected management to keep departments in line with their budgets. He also changed production line techniques in order to meet the varied emotional and personality needs of the employees, accepting the fact that some workers *need* a repetitive task. His feeling was that by tightening controls and assuming greater responsibility and authority, he helped the firm to weather the crisis. The president conceded that the participative management phase, sponsored by the outside consultants, enlarged the work skills of his employees. This fact helped the company's recovery and the president predicted that 1973 would be one of the company's best profit years.

This example proves nothing, but illustrates the complicated relationships that are an inevitable part of the management/consultant interaction. The latent power and authority was made manifest by the crisis, and for the time being, the new hierarchical system seems to be working satisfactorily. Unfortunately, the transition led to the exclusion of the consultants, and no clear lessons can be learned from the experiment.

We have developed the themes of facilitator and interventionist as an essential dimension of the dynamics of

[10]"Where Being Nice to Workers Didn't Work," *Business Week,* 20 January 1973, pp. 99–100.

change. We will discuss the various forms and styles of leadership when discussing systems for change in mental health (therapeutic communities) in Part II.

Identification of Symptoms and/or Goals

No system can move in a purposeful direction until it has identified its problems and goals. To initiate such a process requires motivation to change on the part of the people concerned and particularly on the part of top management. When regularly scheduled meetings have been agreed to, one frequent early problem is ease of communication throughout the system. Communication from authority figures downward is an established part of our culture; the reverse is relatively unfamiliar. To be told by top management to talk freely in a meeting is to enter unfamiliar and unchartered waters, whether in industry, a classroom, a hospital ward, or any other system.

In such a setting the facilitator or interventionist prays for the emergence of a risk taker—someone who will risk sharing his feelings with the group. Given some degree of trust in the system and shared motivation by the group to do some work, a risk taker usually emerges. The interaction (particularly with top management) is watched closely and the quality of the interaction will either enhance or inhibit further communication. If the authority figures show interest and a willingness to listen, so that social learning occurs and change becomes possible, then everyone identifies positively with the risk taker whose image is enhanced. If, however, the risk taker is brushed aside by management, then the message is that although the invitation is to talk freely, the old rules still apply and the meeting has merely a façade of openness. The risk taker, while probably admired by his peers, may anticipate reprisals from above and his job prospects and even his job security may be jeopardized.

Usually an interventionist who is called in to help the system to change already has some awareness of the motivation of the power figures to interact and learn—otherwise he would not have been willing to get involved. A situation like the one described affords him an early opportunity to demonstrate his skill, and at the same time, test the management's willingness to learn. By describing his reaction (as impartially as possible), he can confront the authority figure and make him aware of the mixed message contained in the invitation to meet to talk freely, and the lack of real freedom in the response by the authority. The reaction of the authority figure, the other group members, and the risk taker to the interventionist's input may now determine the whole future course of events. A willingness to interact with the group and listen to their differing perceptions of his performance changes the group's image of itself. Interaction, sharing of information, expression of feeling, and examination of possible outcomes (change) paves the way for increasing use of group process and learning.

If we are faced with an issue concerning, say, low morale and a rising rate of absenteeism, the temptation is to treat these issues as problems calling for some administrative action, e.g., direct middle management to conduct a series of pep talks, or require medical evidence to justify absence from work. But these are basically symptoms of disease and we need to look at what lies behind the symptoms in order to identify the problem. Thus, in an open communication system, with workers encouraged to talk freely, and in the presence of a facilitator or interventionist or both, the symptoms may indicate the workers' lack of job satisfaction due to their lack of identification with the system as a whole. Further interaction may lead to a greater awareness of the problem and how to resolve it. With such global issues as the ones under discussion, the whole system may come under review. This is immensely time consuming, and may call for a strategy in which various tasks are delegated to natural subgroups within the system. Feedback of such relevant information will hasten the administrative group process, but final decision making cannot be bypassed if the process of social learning and change is to continue.

The process of identifying symptoms and then problems in an open system is closely related to goal setting. Thus, in the example discussed above, the issues were sufficiently broad to affect everyone in the system. The values, attitudes, and beliefs of everyone in the system were in question. Was management concerned primarily with material success, e.g., financial rewards, exam passing, staff rather than patient satisfaction, etc., or were social relationships and other worker satisfaction throughout the system also important?

It would seem that in an open system there is a close dynamic relationship between symptoms, problem identification, problem resolution, and goal setting. At this stage, social values become important and setting goals may involve examining the prevailing culture in the system. Admittedly there is some truth in the idea that everyone lives by a double standard: what they appear to be in public and what they know themselves to be in their own minds. This preoccupation with attitudes, values, and beliefs is outside the concerns of most business organizations, but it should have a high priority in education (including families, schools, colleges, medicine, etc.). We will return to this subject when considering social learning.

Shared Decision Making

An open system is a system that employs two-way communication of thoughts and feelings, seeks relevant information as inputs to regularly scheduled meetings, and is open to learning and change. How far it will strive for shared decision making and at what level of the system will depend on the model that evolves and the goals of the organization.

We are assuming that action planning will involve those people who are to carry out the plan, or at least their chosen representatives. This means that every individual who is involved in the action will have an investment in the outcome, because it is in part "his" plan.

There are degrees of sharing in decision making, dependent on many variables. How important is the decision to be made? How much time can be made available? What priority does the boss or bosses put on the decision, etc. A quick decision may be agreed to by the group through lack of interest. Someone proposes a "reasonable" course of action and the group acquiesces rather than muster the energy to analyze the problem in any depth. Or the group may take another form of shortcut by agreeing on a vote. Such a process leads to no real learning and runs the danger of splitting the group. The minority who lose by the voting procedure will not be identified with a successful outcome to the decision; rather, it may consciously or unconsciously work for its failure.

Another pitfall is manipulation of the group or the abuse of power. The director may try to railroad a decision while achieving some semblance of sharing. He may appear to listen to his colleagues and then retain the final decision-making power. How he interprets the preceding group interaction may be highly subjective and his decision (on behalf of the group!) may not be open to question. This is a very common form of "democracy" and a director who operates this way, may when challenged, angrily protest that, after all, the really creative ideas are his! If this *is* true, then a skilled facilitator would help the group to incorporate his ideas so that the group, through interaction, understanding, and interest, comes to see them as "theirs." We might think of this as a "half open" system, in which the director and the power structure sanctions sharing of information and group interaction stops short of sharing the final decision-making power.

Confrontation

An open system implies that anyone, including the director, can be questioned regarding his statements and actions. Clearly, it is much easier and less risky to confront a peer, or someone lower in the pecking order, than a senior. I feel that this freedom to question anyone is mandatory if an open system is to survive and grow. Without this climate of freedom and trust, the hidden agenda may well become more important than the formal agenda. Communication of feeling will occur covertly with one's buddies without any benefit to the system as a whole. Such a growth of underground movements is an inevitable consequence of block in communication, even in a relatively open system. To reverse such a subversive process means some form of confrontation is needed to bring the hidden agenda into the open. If the confrontation concerns an authority figure or the abuse of power, the person or persons who start the process are taking a calculated risk. The tendency is for the group as a whole to watch with interest and often anxiety, but to remain uncommitted bystanders. The risk taker may challenge the words or actions of someone in authority and precipitate his dismissal. This may happen even when the group has been explicitly told to openly express feelings. This is a crisis point in the group's evolution. Can other individuals risk comment on the original risk taker's criticism? If not, then he is left out on a limb and can hope for support and understanding only from his own circle and in private. But his performance as a sacrificial lamb may, under certain circumstances, help the process of growth in the system. To begin with, he has tested the climate of the group and exposed the fiction of open communication. The reaction by the group to his treatment by the authority may harden their determination to strive for a more open system. The authority figure may sense the concern and disapproval of the group, and aided by his own guilt (if present), he may reconsider his behavior and begin to see some advantage to everyone in sharing feelings as well as content.

In a setting of this kind, a natural facilitator or leader may emerge within the group, but an outside consultant or interventionist may be needed. In either case the need is to create a climate of relative trust so that interaction with a view to understanding and social learning replaces any competitive goal of right or wrong. The director requires support and understanding in relationship to his ultimate responsibility and authority within the total system. This accountability factor may well determine his need to control (hire and fire) individuals until he can trust the expression of feeling, decision-making capability, and sharing of power with the group.

The risk taker must also feel the support of at least some of his peers so that he is not in an isolated and vulnerable position and so that other people can help to interpret the problem as not of one "difficult" individual, but one having validity for at least some other group members.

To establish such a climate of relative trust may prove impossible, in which case the authority of the director will go unchallenged (openly), but nothing will be learned. Such crisis situations given favorable circumstances can lead to social learning.

Social Learning

In the introduction to this book, social learning was described as two-way communication motivated by some inner need or stress, leading to the overt or covert expression of feeling, and involving cognitive processes and change. Such learning may relate to the individual, group, or system. Confrontation as already described has the potential for social learning, but this can be realized only in certain circumstances, as when the the attributes of an open system are available, plus a skilled facilitator or interventionist.

To illustrate the concept of social learning, I would like to describe an incident at a community mental health center where I was acting as an outside consultant. This center employed 25 professionals and served an area with a population of 160,000 people.

The team leader and the head of the alcohol and drug programs had learned, by chance, that research money was available for a program in the prevention of drug addiction. Having already done a fairly comprehensive survey of drug usage in the local schools, and believing in the possibility of education using the mass media, they drew up an outline for a research program. Less than a week was available for the writing of a rough draft which was forwarded to the research agency for comment. This step had been requested by them before making formal application. Copies of the rough draft application were distributed to all of the 25 team members, but time did not permit discussion of the research proposal at the weekly staff meeting. Written communication is vastly different from verbal interaction, and the staff felt that something was being imposed on them without an opportunity for discussion. They reacted violently to the written statement. The team members saw an invasion of new staff that would inevitably effect the role of every member of the existing staff. Would the new staff be paid more? Would the existing staff's job security be affected? Would they have to deal with new leaders who were unfamiliar to them? Would the center's character change, and would the social organization, communication, decision-making process, and so on, be disrupted by a sudden increase in personnel?

The team leader was out of town for a few days and he returned to face an angry and hostile team. He tried to explain his point of view at the weekly team meeting. The prospect of a possible half-million dollar grant, which would make possible the realization of some already partly formulated plans for a preventive drug program, seemed too good an opportunity to ignore. So the head of the drug program had helped him to write a hurried rough draft, which if implemented, would have almost doubled the number of professional personnel at the center.

In retrospect we learned that the plan could have been discussed at the weekly staff meeting before being sent off, and even modified to include the group's suggestions. But in the excitement of the moment, this had not been done.

Instead of the acclaim and approval that the team leader had expected, he was roundly criticized for his precipitate action which was out of context with the team culture that deplored unilateral decisions.

In the interaction that followed, the team realized, some members for the first time, that there was nothing final about the rough draft and even if formal application for a grant were recommended by the research authorities, the revision could be a responsibility shared by the whole team.

The team leader and the head of the drug program, for their part, became aware of the misunderstanding and distortion produced by their written statement—the first notice each member of the team had received.

All the questions and fears of the staff were raised at the weekly team meeting, and the interaction resulted in a change in each team member's perception of the incident and an overall change of attitude toward the grant proposal (social learning). In particular, the team leader, who as the main architect of the plan accepted the major responsibility for the incident, described the effect the process had had on him. He was upset because he felt that most people had not read the original draft of the research proposal. Had they done so, there would have been time for them to raise their difficulties with him personally or to have called an emergency meeting. It hurt him to think that the real merit in the proposal had been obscured by negative feelings engendered by misunderstanding, distortion, and distrust.

The team members replied in terms of the inadequacy of written (one-way) communication and began to focus on the nature of communication and decision-making processes within the center. There was an overall attempt to operate as an open system with two-way communication, interaction between staff members, and a shared decision-making process. But on occasion, particularly in times of stress, the team leader was prone to make unilateral decisions, or in varying degrees, bypass a shared decision-making process.

In this particular incident, the team leader felt he had precipitated the crisis by his haste and failure to share the planning with all the team members, as the plan, if implemented, would inevitably affect everyone. At the same time, he raised the question of expediency, a constant source of anxiety to a leader who is subject to pressures from his administrative seniors, a problem which other team members are largely unaware of. There was also the question of creative ideas and spontaneous action, which sometimes suffered in the relatively slow democratic process.

The discussion led to the identification of several problems relating to sharing of power and responsibility. The first priority was seen to be the nature of the decision-making process on the team that lacked consistency and a clear definition. It was agreed by consensus to set aside a day the following week for a workshop to clarify the decision-making process on that team.

This example demonstrates the nature of a learning situation affecting a team of 25 mental health professionals in confrontation with their team leader and a senior colleague. The process of interaction exposed the limitation of written as opposed to verbal communication. The need to evolve a team plan in concert with every team member was demonstrated clearly, and the team leader felt he would not repeat his mistake in the future. The difficulties of the team leader's role in relation to expediency and his special relationship to his senior administrators reminded the team of their relatively sheltered position. Finally, everyone realized that there was no simple formula for decision making and their whole system would have to be examined in relation to this issue at an all-day workshop planned for the following week. This is a good example of learning as a social process.

Social learning process as applied to the school system has to be distinguished from teaching subject matter, the main preoccupation of most schools. Pupils are expected to memorize information for immediate use in exams and for the long-term use of supposedly essential information. Teachers, on the whole, are not eager to become involved in social interaction with their pupils or with their peers. They have little or no training in group dynamics, and in any case, they operate in what is a relatively closed system. Apart from formal faculty meetings, with an agenda usually established by the principal, there is no time set aside for interacting with peers and/or with pupils. In fact, parents fare better, having regularly scheduled meetings with the school staff (P.T.A.). The significance accorded to this meeting is often determined more by the parents' pressure than by staff motivation.

Many educators feel that the school system should strive for much more than the accumulation of knowledge, which all too often has little relevance to problems of living, and so has relatively little interest for the pupils. Social learning could be used extensively by utilizing real classroom situations or situations that exist in the school generally.

Our approach as a consultant team to the school system has been in terms of organization development. First, we sought sanctions from above by approaching the central authorities. By meeting with these people, we could get some awareness of the attitude at the top. To our surprise, the idea of service (referring problem children for "treatment") did not exclude a systems approach. The authorities had some awareness of the need for open systems in schools and were glad to arrange a meeting with the more liberal and open-minded principals, under their umbrella. From this auspicious start, we were able to arrange a visit to the schools whose principals showed a positive attitude toward an open system and change.

At the regularly scheduled faculty meeting, we were afforded an opportunity to meet with the entire staff of several schools and explain our purpose in terms of organization development and our role as possible change agents to help to develop an open system. The fact that we were invited by the principal implied his approval of our involvement, but also tended to identify us as being in his camp.

The next step was usually an invitation to meet with volunteer teachers to talk about the possibility of implementing an open system in at least some classrooms, and even in some aspects of the school system as a whole.

I have given this outline of an O.D. approach to a school system to illustrate the interrelationship and interdependency of social learning process to a total system. Theoretically, we aimed at a social learning experience at the level of the central authority, the administrators within a particular school, the faculty as a whole, a volunteer group of teachers, or teachers and parents, or one or several classrooms.

It is worth noting that the consumer, in this case the pupils, were not involved in the initial planning, and when we did become involved in a classroom interaction, it was never in response to a felt need by the pupils themselves. Had this occurred, we would have responded gladly, but the adult system would never have allowed such a delegation of responsibility and decision-making power to the pupils.

In some cases, we started in one classroom or several classrooms using several resource people to support and train the teacher or teachers so that they themselves could come to feel competent and comfortable in social learning situations. After five years of experience, we have come to prefer several months of weekly seminars with volunteer teachers before venturing into their classrooms. This approach has the added advantage of getting inputs that highlight problems emanating from the system as a whole, and especially from the authority structure. The role of the authority figures in the system is inevitably discussed and the lack of responsibility of the teachers for the values and culture of the school is often made articulate.

Unilateral decisions made by the principal are commonplace, and this creates anxiety and frustration, which makes teachers conceptualize the possibilities and advantages of a more open system. Social learning at this level may affect by contagion the administrative level, which through invitation or by their own initiative, may join the staff seminars. Such an extension of social learning to the administration is enormously helpful. The principal is seen by parents, school council, and the general public as a reflection of the school's goals, beliefs, and values. A change in the staff that does not affect him may have little effect on change in the direction of an open system.

An example may help to clarify the concept of a contagious effect in social learning. Working over a period of years with a group of volunteer teachers in an elementary school, the principal, although positively motivated toward social change, seldom found time to attend the seminars. One day she approached me, and ignoring a colleague,

Jean, who was a co-consultant, took me to her office. She expressed distrust in Jean's ability to handle present, contemporary problems in the classroom, especially those related to racial issues (this school bused black children from a residential area eight miles away). One teacher (A.B.) was particularly concerned about the behavior of blacks in his class and was dissatisfied with the help he was getting from my colleague, Jean. He told the principal he would prefer Mark's help. Mark, a black, was another of our consultant team (there were five of us).

The principal realized that there was no time for interaction as I was already late for my class. Jean had waited outside the principal's office feeling understandably annoyed at being excluded. Hurrying along the corridor, I briefly told her the details and said we would have to discuss the situation at the review after the classes with the volunteer teachers, and I said I hoped the principal would be present.

Unfortunately, the principal found it necessary to cancel the review, as the volunteer teachers were required at a crisis meeting elsewhere. So a week elapsed before we could meet with the five volunteer teachers, the five resource people, and the principal.

I fed back my version of what had happened and was immediately assailed by the teacher, A.B., and the principal, because as they saw it, I had betrayed the principal's trust by informing Jean about the situation. Jean now became angry because she felt that A.B., the teacher with whom she had been working, should have discussed the situation with her rather than run to the principal. I admitted that I should have told the principal that I could not regard her input as confidential, but it was a hurried interaction, and I had expected a review a few hours later when the whole situation could have been discussed.

It became apparent that the consultants and the school system operated on different value systems. The consultants expected open communication based on trust, while the principal, often pressed for time and used to making unilateral decisions, operated in a relatively closed system, and this was expected of her by the teachers.

At first, the teachers were very uncomfortable feeling that the principal's actions and authority were being challenged. It was the principal who sanctioned change and opened up a learning process. She felt that it would have been more effective initially to have both Jean and the teacher, A.B., in the office with me for the few minutes available, or better still to have waited for the review hour when the situation could have been turned into a learning situation. As it was, a week had elapsed and anger had built up among everyone involved in the incident. A.B., used to unquestioning obedience, had expected Mark to replace Jean and had had to interact with his class in the presence of an angry consultant, Jean. Jean could not express her anger in front of the class and as the review had been cancelled (another unilateral decision on the part of the principal), she had to wait a week for the confrontation.

Ever since that time, the principal has openly discussed her tendency to make unilateral decisions. This was seen as a characteristic of any school culture, accepted by teachers as inevitable, and questioned only in private. The confrontation and the principal's willingness to consider a more open system initiated a learning process. But did teachers really want more responsibility, an inevitable accompaniment of shared decision making? And did the school curriculum and the traditional role of the teacher lend themselves to a flexible system? Such a goal of an open system would mean, among other things, many meetings, two-way communication that would often be painful, and a growing awareness of problems among both staff and pupils, which for want of time and/or motivation could be ignored or at least rationalized by the current system.

Another example using the classroom as a subsystem

of the school system may help clarify this concept. When a class is exposed to social learning and given an opportunity to learn problem solving, we are up against the same difficulties a group therapist experiences with a new group. Our experience as a team of consultants over the past four years is very similar to that of Glasser.[11] Seat any class of school children in a circle, away from their formal rows of desks, and there is the anticipation of interaction. However, such an unstructured situation is as anxiety provoking for school children as it is for a new psychiatric patient group or for any other group of people. With school children, the warming up process can be hastened, especially in the younger age groups, by role playing. The goal of such a group is to get children interested in what lies behind behavior so that they can begin to examine their attitude toward their own and other people's behavior. They begin to think for themselves instead of blindly accepting the mores of their peer group and the expectations of their teachers. They may begin a process of re-evaluating many of their traditional cultural values and learning new skills in problem solving. A brief illustration may clarify these points.

A class of nine-year-olds with twenty-five children of both sexes began to discuss a familiar topic: how the sexes differ. The girls complained bitterly about the boys throwing snowballs at them, even though they did not want to play. We decided to develop this theme by recreating the situation by role playing using volunteers. Three little girls left the classroom and returned crying and frightened. They had been set upon by three boys who hit them with snowballs mercilessly. The three boy volunteers now returned to the classroom and the whole class discussed their behavior. The discussion led to the concept of the use of

[11] W. Glasser, *Schools without Failure* (New York: Harper and Row, 1969).

physical force, and the biggest boy in the class was accused, even by peers of his own sex, of abusing his strength. The topic of bullying saved the class from the familiar polarization into boy and girl factions and led to a discussion of the meaning of the "bully's" behavior. He merely emphasized what was a status symbol among the boys, a boy's need to demonstrate his strength and incidentally his "superiority" over girls. Luckily, this boy's peers stressed his good qualities too, and the class agreed to focus on these and devalue his unnecessary use of force. In this supportive setting, one boy pointed out that the "bully" tended to pick on the weaker boys whom he knew could not challenge his strength and so reinforced his own image of a "tough guy."

Our contention is that if the school system would give as much thought and attention to learning as a social process as it does to memorizing subject matter, many problems of later life might be avoided. Educationalists like Neill, Rodgers, Bruner, Glasser, and Silberman have been advocating this approach for many years.[12,13,14,15,16]

Internal Commitment

It goes without saying that social learning and change are directly related to the degree of commitment by those individuals constituting the group or subsystem. "Internal commitment means the course of action or choice that has been internalized by each member so that he experiences a high degree of ownership and has a feeling of responsibility about the choice and its implications. Internal commit-

[12]Neill, *Summerhill.*

[13]Carl R. Rogers, *Freedom to Learn* (Columbus, Ohio: Charles E. Merrill, 1969).

[14]Jerome S. Bruner, *Toward a Theory of Instruction.*

[15]Glasser, *Schools without Failure.*

[16]C. Silberman, *Crisis in the Classroom.*

ment means that the individual has reached the point where he is acting on the choice because it fulfills his own needs and sense of responsibility, as well as those of the system."[17] Argyris sees commitment as an outcome of the individual's considered judgment based on relevant information and free choice.

Briggs gives a striking illustration of internal commitment in his account of a change system in a prison.[18] I acted as consultant during the four years of this project. Sixty felons, young first offenders who volunteered to participate in this experimental program, had been remanded to the California Department of Corrections to serve a minimum of one year in prison. In phase one, they were selected by staff who saw them individually; this covered the first two years of the project. Subsequently, they were selected by a group of residents (prisoners) and usually one staff member.

The setting for this project, the minimum security prison at Chino in southern Califorina, had a history of liberal reform, and the sanctions from above were positive. Given this support, Briggs effected remarkable changes within his experimental unit despite constant friction with the relatively traditional culture of the surrounding prison.

Using a therapeutic community or open system approach, he slowly gained the confidence and trust of the staff (correctional officers concerned with discipline, and correctional counsellors concerned with "treatment") and the residents.

"In the third of these (four) years, the correctional officers had moved into positions at first resembling those of the counsellors. The residents took on the former duties of the officers, ran their own housing unit and supervised

[17] Argyris, *Intervention Theory and Method,* p. 20.

[18] Stuart Whiteley, Dennie Briggs, and Merlyn Turner, *Dealing with Deviants* (New York: Schocken Books, 1973), Ch. 5–6.

their own work projects. They then began to take up the roles of the counsellors and the small-group leaders. There was constant 'role blurring' among the staff and the residents, but in addition, there was movement of roles—role displacement—and a more fluid overall social structure. In the next year—the fourth—the officers became more involved with the administration of the project and acted as 'consultants' for the residents, who in turn were performing roles more like those of the counsellors. The officers were supportive of the men's efforts to try new things and were now able to teach them skills which they themselves had recently acquired, such as leading small groups, interviewing, intervening and using crisis situations, reviewing things they had done, and generally promoting and supporting their ideas. In the final six months of the project, several of the residents took on these things too; they became consultants to the new inmate group coordinators."

The responsibility and power that Briggs, as the project director, had initially to assume was gradually delegated to the system itself. Unilateral decisions by Briggs or other officers gave way to a shared decision-making process with the residents.

The sharing of information became formalized in the social organization. At the daily community meetings of all 60 residents and staff, a new resident was expected to review all his delinquent activities within a week of his arrival at the unit. Another pinpoint meeting was expected of him about midway in his stay: he had to review what he thought he had accomplished and his present plans for the remainder of his stay.

In spite of the fact that these young offenders were prone to violence, no acts of violence with weapons occurred during the four years of the project. At the same time, fistfights were seen as serving a useful purpose as the factors behind the anger were discussed in subsequent meetings, and they enhanced the process of learning.

The residents undertook fire watch duties from 11:00 P.M. to 7:00 A.M., thus allowing all staff to go home at night. In the first two years of the project with constant custodial supervision, five residents escaped from the institution. In the latter two years with total inmate supervision, there were no escapes.

The internal commitment of the residents led to intensive interaction in closed living groups of eight or ten new residents. Along with two group coordinators, men who had volunteered to remain in the project beyond the date of their anticipated discharge and were judged to be skilled in group work, formed a closed living group. This unit was supervised by the community as a whole, but given considerable freedom to learn how to develop their own initiative and establish goals of their own choosing: an active social process as opposed to passive instruction.

The internal commitment achieved by the residents represented a challenge to the professional staff.

"In the approach developed in this project where emphasis was on creating a structure in which individuals could shape social roles, tolerate role conflicts, analyze role performances and both perfect and change role expectations, knowledge of the dynamic forces in individual's behavior could be a hindrance as well as an advantage. In the seminars for the correctional officers, when residents were included, and in the educational courses for the more advanced ones, we were constantly impressed at how quickly so-called non-professionals could grasp sophisticated concepts, translate them into action, observe "interactions" and then return to the seminar with examples for further discussion. They could, more easily than the professionals, keep out technical jargon and explanations, and they were not under the same pressure to talk. They were keen on and highly adept at putting concepts into action and testing them for effect. Unlike the professionals, they could happily abandon an ineffective course, and try something new."[19]

Group Consensus[20]

Compared with internal commitment, consensus is a group reaction. The individual is influenced by the group in a reactive way. We regard consensus as a more sophisticated form of shared decision making. The term implies that the group has spent sufficient time on a particular topic to have worked it through to the point where every individual is ready for action and is internally committed. There is no absolute implied, as it is impossible to "read" a group, or to understand the nature of each individual's internal commitment. Nevertheless, just as in a group psychotherapy session there are times when the group seems to have found a common denominator, and a topic seems to absorb everyone's attention with a general feeling of movement, so a feeling of consensus may emerge. Clearly, we are in a very subjective and arbitrary field. If a leader tests the group climate by expressing *his* feeling that consensus has been reached, the response may not be reliable. For instance, the charismatic effect of the leader is liable to be felt when a topic is being discussed with which the leader is known to be strongly identified. It may be expedient for some group members to support a person rather than a cause or a principle.

Unlike internal commitment, consensus will inevitably call for some degree of compromise in most or all of the individuals concerned. Having had a fair hearing, an individual may decide that his particular emphasis or interest

[19]Whiteley, Briggs & Turner, *Dealing with Deviants.*
[20]Maxwell Jones, 1968a.

has not been incorporated in the group decision, but that he can go along with the general goal. If this goal violates the position of any one member, then consensus can only apply to a group that has reached a high degree of openness and trust. It is a very important dimension in the dynamics of change.

To attempt to reach consensus on minor issues is probably a waste of time. Effective organization development implies skill in determining when to use more simple techniques of shared decision making and when to spend time, energy, and skill on reaching consensus.

Timing is another important aspect of consensus. When I was the medical superintendent of a mental hospital in Scotland, I felt that on important issues, consensus was essential before taking action. This belief was shared by my colleagues, and so if consensus could not be reached, the issue was left on the table. It might not be reopened for months, or it might be forgotten altogether. If the former, it usually meant that the motivation to work through the issue had returned, and changed circumstances (more relevant information, greater public pressure, a change in priorities, etc.) might now lead to consensus. If the latter, then a process of natural selection and growth within the system was being followed. This evolutionary process has the virtue of keeping interest at the highest possible level, and seems to me to epitomize the concept of an open system with the maximum likelihood for change. What has already been discussed under Chapter 1, The Dynamics of Change indicates the various checks and balances inherent in an effective model for change. The direction of change may depend on a skilled facilitator or interventionist to help the system to identify symptoms and define goals. I feel that aiming for consensus on important issues will ensure commitment, interest, social learning, and change in a carefully explored direction.

Another aspect of consensus concerns the level at

which the interaction occurs. Assuming that the problem or decision is of sufficient importance to the group to justify an attempt to reach consensus, then what level of involvement is called for? If the issue concerns a simple practical problem, like the number of toilets required for a new geriatric unit, it will call for surface interaction between the group members. If other variables such as competing claims for the money available become manifest, then the feelings and attitudes of the competing subgroups must be examined. This working through of intra and interpersonal issues can be very time consuming. It is here that the skill of the leader or leaders (facilitators) is all important. To leave important issues unresolved, lowers morale and may lead to splinter groups and feelings of impotence in the total group. On the other hand, to work through all interpersonal differences may be impossibly time consuming. It is probably wise to intervene at a level no deeper than that which the energy and resources of the group can afford. Here the skill of the facilitator may help the group to decide on the level at which problem solving and system change can most profitably be attempted.

Action

We have covered the main preliminary essentials to action, but there is always the possibility that action planning has been faulty. This may show up only when the plan is being tried out. In an open system, reconsideration (recycling) of the plan should not be difficult, but this does not apply in a relatively closed system.

In a junior high school, six consultants met with twelve volunteer teachers, in addition to three counselors and the assistant principal, for six weeks. The school system had been known to me for over two years. The group, after much discussion, decided that they were ready to interact with the pupils with a view to sharing responsibility for discipline in the 12 classrooms.

One resource person went with each of the volunteer teachers to interact with the class. The results were far from satisfactory. The time selected was one when teachers had been free to develop special interests with the pupils. The pupils had not been identified with the planning of our project, and although forewarned of our intentions, started with no investment in the outcome. Following the class, the teachers and consultants met for an hour to review the interaction in various classes, and pupils were invited to attend this review if they wished.

It soon became apparent that in most of the classes the pupils were acting out their resentment to an imposed topic (class discipline). They felt that they would prefer to spend the time doing their homework, or following the special interest subjects that had been suspended to make room for the new topic. Moreover, the pupils seemed disinterested in self-discipline and preferred to gripe about adult injustices and unfairness than assume responsibility themselves. Scapegoating the adults in the system gave them a considerable degree of satisfaction and reinforced their passive aggressive position—a familiar attribute of any school culture.

The teachers, too, became angry and frustrated. They blamed the consultants and assistant principal for being manipulated into a role for which they were unprepared. All this we could verify from our involved position as consultants. We had spent far too short a time in preparing the volunteer teachers for their role. We had assumed consensus on the part of the teachers to the topic of class discipline, but had not taken the time or trouble to assure relevant information gathering. But the failure to involve the pupils in the planning stages was a fatal error for which we paid dearly.

We were forced to reconsider our plan and leave each

classroom to identify its own problems and set its own goals. Three months elapsed between our original staff meeting and our reconstituted program involving the pupils in the process. This failure in planning and premature action highlighted the strength of the cultural factor in schools. The pupils are seldom involved in planning in things that matter to them—curriculum, homework, discipline, etc. This in no way excuses the failure of experienced consultants who overlooked the involvement of pupils in the planning, but it taught them the danger of being seduced into accepting the norms of a system.

Chapter 4

EVALUATIVE OR EVOLUTIONARY PHASE

The outcome of planned action will give the best index of the effectiveness of the system. But the effectiveness of an open system will also be judged by its effect on the individuals comprising the system. Has their job satisfaction increased; has their potential for growth been realized, including their potential for leadership? Do they now enjoy better relationships with their peers, with greater sharing of feelings, and more mutual support? Do they identify with the boss, and at the same time feel better understood by others? Above all, do they identify with and operate as an active part of the organization?

It seems to me that a group identity is one essential component of a healthy personality. We all need a reliable support system, otherwise we are liable to feel isolated and vulnerable. To feel a strong identity with one's peer group in an open system means an opportunity to evaluate constantly one's attitudes, values, and beliefs. This, in turn, leads to a feeling of self-growth with new and wider perspectives.

An open system also leads to the identification of symptoms and affords at least a partial methodology for overcoming these. Nothing succeeds like success and such experiences inevitably enhance one's positive self-image.

In a world where competition is often fierce and success may require the defeat of a rival, it is an infinite relief to most people to watch a system grow and to feel oneself a part of that evolution.

The concept of a therapeutic community, an early model for change in psychiatric systems, laid great stress on a democratic, egalitarian authority structure, as opposed to the traditional hierarchical structure.[1] Leadership tended increasingly to become multiple, irrespective of professional training, and leaders emerged according to their aptitude in any particular situation.

At the stage of action planning, various criteria can be discussed that will indicate outcome. Failure to reach certain objectives may indicate flaws in the program and call for a recycling of the plan. This was indicated in our example of a junior high school when the expected interaction between pupils and adults for effecting class discipline failed to materialize.

An open system seems to be a prerequisite for an organization to change. To identify its symptoms and goals, an organization must go through a long process of interaction and social learning. The inherent capacity of an organization to change and grow on its own will depend on many variables, including the quality of the staff, their professional training, and above all, their willingness to change.

To attempt program evaluation, we must know what we are attempting to accomplish. If in a social system of say 50 employees, we might hope to open communication, develop a process of social learning, and aim at decision making by consensus. Then we could measure open communication with some precision. But the latter two

[1]Maxwell Jones, *The Therapeutic Community.*

goals would present tremendous difficulties because of their abstract nature.

A questionnaire to all fifty employees at the end of the intervention might produce useful information on all three goals. The same applies to interviews of all the personnel. In addition, a process observer, preferably from within the system, can complement the above information. Videotapes store information for future study and can capture someting of the process of change, e.g., filming an administrative meeting at timed intervals will help to measure change in all three areas, and in particular, help to capture the abstractions of the latter two.

The examples of change given in this book fall into three categories: (a) short-term consultation visits, lasting up to two weeks, in which an attempt to facilitate change using the techniques already described is made either alone or at times in conjunction with a colleague (b) regularly scheduled visits often two or three hours a week for as long as one year or longer, and (c) the evolutionary model, e.g., the one in which the author was the medical director (Henderson Hospital, 1947–1959 and Dingleton Hospital, 1962–1969) and functioned as a facilitator of group process. Bob Rapoport and a team of seven behavioral scientists attempted to evaluate the process of change at Henderson Hospital over a period of three years.[2] At Fort Logan Denver, Colorado, a voluminous research program has helped to "strengthen" the largely descriptive accounts of the open system used there.[3,4]

[2]Robert Rapoport, *Community as Doctor* (Springfield, Ill.: Charles C. Thomas, 1960).

[3]Ethel M. Bonn, "A Therapeutic Community in an Open State Hospital; Administrative Therapeutic Links," *Hospital and Community Psychology,* 20(1969):269–78.

[4]S. B. Schiff, "A Therapeutic Community in an Open State Hospital: Administrative Framework for Social Psychiatry," *Hospital and Community Psychiatry* 20(1969):259–68.

I would now like to give a concrete example of accountability (cost effectiveness) and am indebted to my collaborators at Bethesda Community Mental Health Center, John DeHaan and Tom Barrett.

Can an Open System be Evaluated?

The question which each organization should answer is whether open systems are compatible with accountability.

During the three years when efforts were made to decrease the authoritarian decisions and to increase the amount of staff participation, additional resources were added but productivity did not increase. Inpatient beds were reduced from twenty to ten, enabling the Center to shift $100,000 to non-hospital programs and thereby increase staff. In addition, three staff members were added from a special alcohol grant ($36,000) with no apparent increase in productivity. In fact, during the first six months of our third year of open systems, productivity decreased by 1,000 interviews as compared with the previous year (10% decrease).

The decrease in productivity can be viewed by several other methods. During fiscal year 1971–72, our cost per client contact was $16.49. During fiscal year 1973–74, our cost had risen to $27.32 per client contact.

If our center had been reimbursed by National Health Insurance, instead of a staffing grant, at the rate of $25.00 per individual and family contact and $15.00 per group contact, we probably would have been bankrupt by July of 1974. During the 1971–72 fiscal year we would have earned a profit of $1,457 and by the 1973–74 fiscal year we would have a loss of $154,000.

It was not uncommon during 1973–74 for a staff member to record one to three persons seen a day. Some called this period of our existence, Country Club Management; staff doing what they wanted to, how they wanted to, and when they wanted to.

Chris Argyris, in his book, *Intervention Theory and Method,* implies that a system is healthy if it is able to: (1) generate valid information, (2) exert freedom of choice, and (3) manifest internal commitment to the decisions made.

Since our staff appeared to be relatively healthy it seemed reasonable to expect that they would accept accountability as a guide to greater effectiveness and productivity.

One of the major problems appeared to be a lack of valid information about the productivity problems our organization was facing.

During June of 1973 the staff agreed to begin filling every thirty minutes our activities sheets, which coded the programs they were participating in. Once a month, this information was computerized and we received a monthly printout that was twenty-four inches long, twenty inches wide, and one inch thick. Productivity continued to decrease. We found too much information can be as useless as too little information.

During this same time some referral sources began to complain that some clients were not really being helped when they came to our organization, which prompted us to send out customer satisfaction cards, if the therapist remembered to fill them out at the time of entry.

By January of 1974 it became apparent that our organization was continuing to deteriorate on the accountability issue. Also during January a full-time program evaluator was hired who compelled us to face the question of what valid information would really be useful.

Looking back, the answers we came up with appear to be quite simple. All we needed to know was how effective the therapists were, and how much it cost us to have them provide the service.

Our non-computerized management information system contained two basic pieces of information on every therapist, every month: cost and effectiveness.

Cost is determined by allocating operating and administrative costs to departments according to an accounting formula. Salaries are then used to distribute these overhead costs to therapists within each department. The total of the salary and the allocated overhead is the complete monthly cost for each individual therapist. The number and type of each therapist's treatment sessions are then accumulated along with the total number of clients in these sessions. Both of these figures are divided into the monthly cost figure resulting in cost per session and cost per person figures for all therapists and all departments. For the first month cost per person seen ranged from $8.00 per person to $150.00 per person.

Staff reaction to the new information system was mixed. Some claimed we had lost all interest in quality. Others felt a marked deterioration in freedom. Most said the new information system was producing inaccurate figures, and they were right to some extent but the figures weren't that far from the truth.

By February, the staff agreed that each program area would get a monthly management information report (which contained the basic productivity and cost information as described above) and then each department could use it as they wanted.

This was to be the beginning of a six month effort to develop uniform acceptance of the new management information system. The departments which utilized the information rapidly decreased their cost. The departments which down-graded the management information system continued to have high cost figures until peer pressure was felt.

During March our program evaluator began to develop outcome data for the effectiveness part of our information system. This data came primarily from a good attainment scaling system modeled after the Goal Attainment Scale (G.A.S.) system in the Program Evaluation Project in Minnesota headed by Dr. Tom Kiresuk.[5] As a part of this system intake workers who have been trained in G.A.S. evaluate each client's goals as he enters treatment and completes a follow-up interview after termination to determine how much progress has been made on each goal. The procedure is objectified as much as possible to eliminate possible bias. For example, levels are determined at intake so that a client's goal level is firmly established before treatment and before the follow-up interview is completed. Additionally, the workers who complete the G.A.S. are not involved in the therapy process. Goals are reviewed regularly by the team of intake workers and the program evaluator. Termination status and pre and post profile scores are used to supplement the G.A.S. outcome data.

A marriage between open systems and accountability seemed to have developed in our mental health center by August of 1974. We were beginning to see the corrective actions taking place. Production from January 1974 to July of 1974 had shown a 20 percent increase and client-drop-out rates were declining rapidly. Staff was now open to having promotions based on a cost effectiveness model instead of a time served model. Looking back on the three year span of time, it appears that we began with a form of management which had some resemblence to an autocracy.

Our second stage of development was marked by turbulance and some impoverishment. During this time, role

[5]Thomas J. Kiresuk and Robert E. Sherman, "Goal Attainment Scaling. A General Method for Evaluating Community Mental Health Programs," *Community Mental Health Journal,* 4:6(1968): 443–53.

identity crises were common and there was a lack of responsibility. We began asking ourselves, "Who has the power?" We decided that when you are disorganized, no one has the power.

The current stage of our management is characterized by an accountable democracy in which individual, department and organizational responsibility have been clearly identified by means of key indicators (valid information).

It is our belief that open systems and accountability are compatible. In addition, we speculate that it may be possible to avoid many of the problems our organization encountered during our turbulent stage of management, if key indicators of responsibility are clearly identified *before* efforts are made to transfer responsibility downward.

The staff has made a major investment in improving our accountability. They not only have been effective in improving our accountability, they also have accomplished this improvement while maintaining the positive feelings and cohesiveness of the staff at the same time.

An open system can be accountable if valid information is available to them.

Chapter 5

GENERAL CONSIDERATIONS

In the Introduction we drew attention to the present dilemma in which psychiatry finds itself; should it continue in its traditional form based on the ideas of "sickness," pathology and treatment, or should it widen its scope to embrace some of the social issues of our time? To this we may add the functions of a change agent and the whole field of prevention and the betterment of health generally.

It seems reasonable to assume that the social organization to which an individual belongs can help or hinder the evolution of that individual's full potential for growth. Indeed, this is the major emphasis of this book.

A recent report issued by the U.S. Federal Government indicates that industry generally is in serious trouble.[1] Working conditions, says the report, have dehumanized

[1]U.S. Department of Health Education and Welfare, *Work in America* (Cambridge, Mass.: Massachusetts Institute of Technology, 1972).

the workers, with the accompanying social ills of increasing absenteeism, high worker turnover rates, and decreased family stability. To these social ills the report adds: increased incidence of mental illness, abuse of alcohol and drugs, together with aggression and deliquency in the work setting and in society at large.

The behavioral science team who were contracted to do the study felt that the major cause of these problems was the lack of involvement of the mass of employees in the communication and decision-making processes of their particular firm. The employees felt that their only incentive to work was their pay packet. Work which took up most of their lives was a relatively meaningless exercise and did little or nothing to enhance their self-image, and even less to help stimulate growth and social maturity.

A social systems approach to change may be valid, but as yet this position lacks proof and relies largely on experimental evidence. Workers in the organizational development field are still largely behavioral scientists. There tends to be a basic assumption that open social systems are "good" and closed systems are "bad." This is clearly an oversimplification, but the mass of evidence points that way if we limit ourselves to the behavioral science literature. But such professionals are already biased by the very nature of their training. They are politically and ideologically liberal, and their work calls for a critical examination of the status quo. Their approach to social problems results in a need to find answers to the symptoms of social distress, and hence, the growth of O.D. and concepts of systems change. But change threatens most social organizations and particularly the control exercised by the power at the top. Not surprisingly, this approach is unwelcome in the Soviet Union and other controlled political systems, be they national, regional, or local.

But apart from a minority of educated "liberals," does the mass of society want change? The evidence seems to point the other way. The United States, which undoubtedly trains more behavioral scientists than any other country, has a federal administration that may go down in history as one of the best (or worst) examples of a closed system in history. Power is centralized to an extraordinary degree and is controlled by fewer people than is the case in the Soviet Union. In addition, the electorate has indicated that most of its members prefer this system of control to a more open system with greater delegation of responsibility and power.

We are left with a dilemma; frustrated, disillusioned, and unfulfilled individuals, who appear to be in the majority in most parts of the world, see the social unrest around them and seem to call for social change, while society seems to be unwilling to face the effort, distress, and insecurity that inevitably accompanies social change. This dilemma would appear to be one of the root causes of the present scourge of drug and alcohol addiction, particularly in young people. During the past decade they rebelled, often violently, against the mores of their elders, only to find that social change could not be easily attained. Lacking clear goals, powers, or the skills needed to effect systems change, they have tended to reconcile themselves to more individual types of change, e.g., dress, hair style, etc., or simply have tended to conform to the existing culture for reasons of job security and career advancement. For some, particularly the socially disadvantaged, the dilemma has resulted in feelings of helplessness and hopelessness, the only recourse being to escape through drugs, alcohol, mental illness, or suicide.

Where, if at all, does psychiatry fit into this picture? For some, the answer seems to be along lines similar in many respects to the behavioral science organization development approach, but here we have to make a distinction between what has been called community psychology and community mental health.[2] Murrell defines social psychology as "the area within the science of psychology that *studies* the transactions between social system networks, populations, and individuals; that *develops* and *evaluates* intervention methods which improve person-environment 'fits'; that *designs* and *evaluates* new social systems; and from such knowledge and change seeks to *enhance* the psychosocial opportunities of the individual."[3]

Thus, the familiar distinction between psychology and psychiatry, i.e., the study of human behavior compared to the study of pathological behavior is retained in a community context. The Community Mental Health Act passed by Congress in 1963 sanctioned, indeed insisted on, community involvement over and beyond the familiar doctor-patient treatment situation in hospitals, clinics, or offices. For some mental health professionals, this message, while relatively new, meant a geographical change of focus with professional skills and training being shared with "caretakers" in the community such as policemen, ministers, probation officers, teachers, welfare officers, etc. For others, the focus shifted from pathology to social environment and ecology: the interaction between man and his environment. While the impact of social forces on individuals can be linked to the idea of illness as in, say, the development of schizophrenia, or the need for family group therapy, it meant for some an escape from the limiting concept of "illness." It seemed that the path was clear to pay attention to the way in which social systems might assume responsi-

[2]I. Iscoe and C. Spielberger, eds., *Community Psychology: Perspectives in Training and Research* (New York: Appleton-Century Crofts, 1970), The Emerging Field of Community Psychology in Iscoe and Spielberger.

[3]Stanley A. Murrell, *Community Psychology,* p. 23.

bility for psychosocial growth, and the development of the latent potential in individuals. Here the preoccupation is with health rather than with illness.

For psychiatrists and mental health professionals generally, the move to community involvement in the social environment of the patient was an enormous step. It emphasized their limitations when separated from the hospital or office setting, which enhanced their own self-image, but which tended to sap the patient's self-confidence and place him in a dependent relationship with the professional. But his function was still the familiar one of therapist, even though the circumstances (interacting in a community setting) might blur the distinction between treater and treated, and call for a new awareness of the importance of socioeconomic status, education, and culture, which tended to blunt his psychotherapeutic tools.

The mental health professional has, to date, trained and operated in a system geared to the treatment of "sick" individuals, whether in the hospital or in the community. Now, some of these workers are tending to leave the community mental health field and become involved in social systems in order to try to enhance the opportunities for individuals to realize their latent potential by being part of a system that furthers psychosocial growth. To call this preventive psychiatry is to imply that the primary goal of a systems approach in this context is the prevention of illness. A more positive goal would seem to be the furtherance of health, although there is an inherent complementarity between the two emphases.

If we follow the path of trying to effect psychosocial growth in a social system, we are immediately faced with the problem of operating in a system to which we usually do not belong and which may have no interest in change. In the mental health system, we tend to assume that the "sick" person is motivated to change in the direction of "wellness." This assumption may be invalid, but the goal of "wellness" has a positive connotation and the whole system is organized to achieve this end. Also, the mental health professional has power, status, and credibility within the system.

A community psychology program aimed at psychosocial growth in individuals within the system and a social organization that is flexible and open to change implies a totally different function for the professional. He no longer can depend on his credibility—in fact to be identified as, say, a psychiatrist, may hinder his acceptance by the social system which has no wish to be "treated," and has as yet no capacity to identify its problems or even want to change. At best, he may gain entrance to the system in response to its awareness, no matter how vague, that something is wrong and outside help is needed.

Outside help may gain credibility in the light of professional training and the professional may be accorded the status of consultant. But it is still outside help and subject to distrust from the insiders who will judge the outsider on the merits of his performance.

From the start, the role of the outside consultant is a difficult one and the professional cannot fall back on a supportive system of which he is a part, as was the case, say, in his hospital days. In addition, the question inevitably arises—what is he selling? Everyone is presumably afraid of death, and the medical profession has developed and prospered as a result. A doctor has no need to sell himself where illness is concerned, provided he has the necessary training and skill. But the same person trying to sell community psychology or to change social systems in an attempt to realize the full potential of the individuals comprising that system, can expect trouble. Medicine has credibility and is understood by most people as the best available antidote for sickness.

Much of the power of the medical profession may be based on trust and belief which, at times, amounts to witchcraft, but its accomplishments in general are capable of proof, a position that the behavioral scientist must envy.

The consultant or change agent in social systems has relatively little credibility, because he operates on the belief that an open system is, in many cases, better than a closed system, and that any organization can be helped to change. But for what purpose, and what guarantees are there that the results will be more positive than negative?

The specter of the abuse of power is undoubtedly in people's minds when confronted with the possibility of social change initiated from outside. The outside consultant can justify his presence if he is called in by a social organization in response to a need, e.g., increased absenteeism or an excessive turnover of staff. The emerging technology already described can then be invoked, the problem identified, and a solution attempted. But this brings us back full circle to the concept of pathology and "treating" the symptoms, even though we are considering social systems rather than "sick" individuals.

Without a demonstrable need for change, can we expect people to believe in concepts like organization development? Are we (consultants) attempting to manipulate people into a new social order on the basis of our experiential evidence, which lacking hard research data, may be little more than an article of faith? Are we even motivated primarily by our goals of social benefits to the system, or by personal profit motives and ultimately a desire for power?

To many thinking people, behavioral scientists are viewed with suspicion. By what authority are they aspiring to infiltrate into social systems as potential change agents? What are their credentials?

I have stressed these doubts because I too share them. But apart from the aura of medicine and the inherent belief that many people have in the doctor/patient relationship, is the plight of psychiatry fundamentally different? Admittedly, we have evolved treatment methodologies that are based on the "pathology" of the "sick" person and the "treatment" role of the psychiatrist. But psychotherapeutic methods have failed to produce impressive results, and the proliferation of different treatment methodologies suggests the failure of any one method to win general acceptance.

Having expressed our reservations about the effectiveness of the "treatment" approach to pathology, whether in the individual or social systems dimension, how can we attempt to justify the much newer and less tried and tested field of community psychology which attempts to improve the opportunities for psychosocial growth in a social system?

The fact is that this approach is as yet largely idealistic and lacks factual evidence for its effectiveness. But the evolution of new systems cannot occur unless people are prepared to take risks and develop new models of systems, the effectiveness of which can later be studied and researched.

The therapeutic community concept was such a model and originally developed as a reaction to the hierarchical closed systems that typified psychiatric facilities in the 1950s.[4] The concept was an early attempt to develop an open system at a time when systems theory as we know it now was nonexistent. A team of behavioral scientists studied the structure and function of the theory, but reached no very definite conclusions.[5]

Nevertheless, like psychotherapy itself, this approach to change continued to create interest and many models of therapeutic communities, often very dissimilar, have evolved in the United States and in Europe.

In this context, let me suggest with trepidation that new models for social interaction and change can be justi-

[4]Jones, *The Therapeutic Community.*
[5]Rapoport, *Community as Doctor.*

fied if they represent an internal commitment to developing a system that *may* result in more people developing their full potential as creative individuals. The necessary corollary to this position is that the organization is both willing and eager to have its operation studied, researched, and evaluated.

Examples of such models can be quoted from the field of education, where A. S. Neill's Summerhill and many of the new "open" or "free" elementary schools are creating controversy, interest, and research.[6,7] Many teachers are beginning to realize that how they teach and how they act may be more important than what they teach.

Critics of these models of an open system may well say that A. S. Neill imposed his will on the teachers, pupils, and parents at Summerhill, and I have lived with this criticism of my several attempts to develop a therapeutic community or open system over the past 26 years.

This attitude on the part of outsiders has much validity, except that the outsider cannot fully assess what has gone on inside the system and is no more objective than the innovator or creator of the system is from his inside position. So where does the truth lie?

In an attempt to gain at least a degree of objectivity, we have already discussed the concept of a facilitator. Unlike an O.D. consultant or interventionist who already is identified with a systems approach and responds to a felt need to observe the system, help to identify the problem, work it through with the personnel involved, and then leave, the facilitator has a different function.

He may already be a member of the social system, possibly the creator or a resource person who has status and credibility. He is not a leader with power and authority as this would immediately destroy his function, which is

[6]Neill, *Summerhill.*

[7]Silberman, *Crisis in the Classroom.*

basically to help the system to help itself. The simplest example is if the creator of a system became convinced that an open system would benefit everyone in the social organization, then he would delegate responsibility and authority to those individuals who were appropriate for such leadership roles. Theoretically, he might make his job redundant in terms of power and leadership, but would be in an ideal position to help the system to help itself. His presence as a tried and trusted member of the system would mean that his experience and skills were available without the power to enforce his ideas in the face of resistance or doubt on the part of his colleagues. The learning process would take priority over getting his own way. But his experience in dealing with outside agencies, confronting colleagues, identifying hidden agendas, establishing priorities, etc. would be available to the system.

To many this may sound unreal, but after being the physician superintendent at Dingleton Hospital in Melrose, Scotland for seven years, I felt that I was largely redundant as far as formal authority, unilateral decision making, hiring and firing, and the goals of the institution were concerned. I had no doubt about my value as a facilitator in helping the system to help itself. At this point in the social evolution of Dingleton, had I tried to make a unilateral decision, I would have had considerable difficulty in reestablishing my position as facilitator. We are talking about an evolutionary process of change toward an open system that covered seven years. The internal commitment of the senior staff to whom the decision-making power had been delegated was of a high order. Decision making by consensus was an established practice in relation to all major problems.

It would be foolish to presume that in the role of facilitator I was completely objective. It is generally accepted that there is no such thing as a basic truth in human relations and no ultimate knowledge. By entering a social system, any one individual changes that system. He can never be truly objective because he cannot know exactly where other people are in terms of their thinking, feelings, or even their use of words.

We are talking in relative terms and struggling to understand the dynamics of change in relation to a more open and flexible system, with particular reference to the use and abuse of power.

In the earlier discussion of the dynamics of change, I tried to outline a theoretical framework to explain the process of change in relation to an open system. We moved from the idea of leadership, in the preliminary or team-building phase, to that of a facilitator or interventionist in the process phase. Now we are exploring the possibility of power, leadership, authority, and responsibility being distributed throughout the system. The crux of this argument seems to me to be in the metamorphosis of the innovator/leader with power and credibility to that of facilitator without the ultimate power that has been redistributed throughout the system. History points to endless examples of creative power leading to change, but the new system is maintained by further use of power and may die with the disappearance of the leader. Alternatively, the leader may reflect the needs of the system of which he is a part, and the system willingly invests the trust and authority in one person. Such a system may evolve even after the disappearance of the formal leader. But a new leader or leaders must be found and will they also reflect the group's needs? This oversimplified comparison points to the need for a social evolutionary process by which the system becomes self-perpetuating and multiple leadership emerges, with shared goals and an identity with the system rather than individual power. In this way, we envisage the possiblity of a flexible system in which open communication and learning as a social process can be maintained. Theoretically, this represents a system of checks and balances in which internal commitment, shared goals, and sensitivity to the outside world can be maintained.

Finally, I would argue that the present-day crisis presented by our technological growth, which has far outstripped our social and political growth, so that we have the atomic stockpile of weapons that could destroy every inhabitant on earth several times over, calls for some immediate policy of change on a global scale.[8]

There is reason to believe that in the United States a counterculture, or a revolt against the values of a society dominated by economic considerations, competition, and a nationalistic aggression that condones war but ignores the needs of the underpriviledged or the racial minorities, is already leading to a new value system particularly apparent in the youth of America.[9] Jean-Francois Revel, a Frenchman who sees this world revolution already starting in the United States, has this to say:

> The "hot" issues in America's insurrection against itself, numerous as they are, form a cohesive and coherent whole within which no one issue can be separated from the others. These issues are as follows: a radically new approach to moral values; the black revolt; the feminist attack on masculine domination; the rejection by young people of exclusively economic and technical social goals; the general adoption of non-coercive methods in education; the acceptance of the guilt for poverty; the growing demand for equality; the rejection of an authoritarian culture in favor of a critical and diversified culture that is basically new, rather than adopted from the old cultural stockpile; the rejection both of the spread of American power abroad and of foreign policy; and a determination that the natural environment is more important than commercial profit.[10]

[8]Toffler, *Future Shock.*

[9]Charles A. Reich, *The Greening of America* (New York: Random House, 1970).

[10]Jean-Francois Revel, *Without Marx or Jesus* (Garden City, N.Y.: Doubleday, 1971).

It is interesting to note that Revel sees the prerequisites of a successful revolution, i.e., a new social system that will survive, in terms of five categories: (a) a critique of the injustice existing in economic, social, and racial relationships; (b) a critique of management, directed against the waste of material and human resources; (c) a critique of political power; (d) a critique of culture—the values and beliefs of the society; (e) a critique of the old civilization-as-sanction or a vindication of individual freedom.

Political theory and systems theory are hard to reconcile, but what Reich calls "consciousness three" and Revel calls "the second world revolution" can, at least in part, be understood in terms of the systems theory which I have attempted to outline. The identification of problems and a methodology that will help in resolving them in an embryonic stage of development. At best, it can only be one factor in implementing the process of change. But the urgency of the crisis for existence on earth seems to justify any approach that may enhance our understanding of the dynamics of change.

Part II

A SYSTEMS APPROACH TO HEALTH AND MENTAL HEALTH INSTITUTIONS

In Part I of this book we have examined some of the general principles of systems theory. I would like now to consider this approach as it applies to mental health institutions. As early as 1947, a psychiatric facility was evolving as a social system and the term therapeutic community came into being.[1] This was essentially an early attempt to evolve an open system, as a reaction against the traditional closed systems of psychiatric hospitals.

[1]Jones, *The Therapeutic Community.*

Chapter 6

SOCIAL ORGANIZATION—THERAPEUTIC COMMUNITIES

The social structure of a therapeutic community is characteristically different from the more traditional hospital. The term implies that the whole community of staff and patients is involved, at least partly, in treatment and administration. The extent to which this is practicable or desirable will depend on many variables, including the attitude of the leader and the other staff, the type of patients being treated, and the sanctions afforded by higher authority. The emphasis on free communication in and between both staff and patient groups and on permissive attitudes that encourage free expression of feeling imply a democratic, egalitarian rather than a traditional hierarchical social organization.

Staff and patient roles and role relationships are the subject of frequent examination and discussion. This is devised to increase the effectiveness of roles and sharpen the community's perception of them. The aim is to achieve sufficient role flexibility so that the role at any one time reflects the expectations of behavior of both staff and patients collectively.

The examination and clarification of roles inevitably sharpens the role prescription but may at the same time lead to some role blurring. This is not contradictory. Thus, it may seem appropriate for nurses as well as social workers to visit patients' homes. The former might accompany patients on home visits to help start the rehabilitation process in the outside world and to encourage the family member to attend ward group meetings. The social worker might visit the home with the patient's approval but not in his presence. The visit might be mainly to try to engage the family members in treatment which would be complementary to the patient's treatment in hospital. Any other role prescription might emerge as a result of discussion with the team.

The overall culture in a ward or psychiatric unit represents the accumulation through time of the attitudes, beliefs, and behavior patterns, common to a large part of the unit. This is arrived at as a result of considerable inquiry into the nature of these attitudes and an attempt is made to modify them to meet the treatment needs of the patients. In this context the term therapeutic culture is sometimes used. The tendency is for these cultural patterns to be most clearly established in the more stable and permanent members of the community, i.e., the staff.

Examples of such attitudes contributing to a therapeutic culture of treatment ideology would be an emphasis on active rehabilitation, as against custodialism and segregation; democratization in contrast to the old hierarchies and formalities of status differentiation; permissiveness in contrast to the stereotyped patterns of communication and behavior; and communalism as opposed to highly specialized therapeutic roles often limited to the doctor.[2]

[2]Rapoport, *Community as Doctor.*

A basic aspect of the social organization of a therapeutic community is the establishment of daily community meetings. By a community meeting, I mean a meeting of the entire patient and staff population who are working together in a single geographical area. I have found it practicable to hold meetings of this kind with as many as 50 patients and 20 to 30 staff. The term group therapy as opposed to community therapy is used in the more conventional sense.[3] A relatively small group of patients who are treated by their own doctor or therapist in a group setting will often represent a subgroup of the total community who have been selected on clinical grounds, age, intelligence, motivation, etc. In my experience, it is desirable for community meetings to be followed by group meetings. In the community meetings, the tensions in the ward or unit at a particular time will be ventilated and will activate a great deal of material within the individual patient. Many of the tensions cannot easily be worked through in a community meeting, but if this is followed by a group meeting, it seems to act as a useful stimulus to communication in the smaller meeting.

The Community Meeting

A ward or treatment unit of, say 20 to 50 patients have to live together, and although, of course, they split into smaller subgroups or even withdraw to a relatively isolated position, the patients must inevitably interact with each other in varying degrees. In a community meeting the staff is exposed to some of the social forces that normally operate on the ward. Harry Wilmer has described in great detail

[3]Henry Walton, ed., *Small Group Psychotherapy* (Middlesex, England: Penguin Books, 1971).

ward meetings of this kind involving very disturbed schizophrenic patients.[4]

The first problem to consider is the attitude of the staff. In general, they will view this type of meeting with very mixed feelings. The charge nurse, or charge aide, may see this as depriving her of her cherished exclusive daily interview with the doctor which, in the past, may have done much to relieve her of her own anxieties. In the past she often became "the therapist" of the ward, describing activities of a disturbing kind to the doctor and recommending "treatment" which not infrequently he was only too glad to accept, failing to realize that the "treatment" he was sanctioning was sometimes relieving the anxiety of the nurse rather than the patient.

Thus, the decision-making power regarding the use of shock treatment or sedatives or transfer of patients to another ward has frequently been centralized in the nursing role. The attitudes of other staff members, although obviously important, may never have been examined, and especially the more junior aides may have come to feel that they were excluded from much of the interest in the work and that their own status was devalued. However, the establishment of a daily community meeting does very little to improve the situation if the staff, other than the doctor, feel that it is a waste of time, and it is liable to create more, rather than less, disturbance among the patients. The charge nurse or aide may find that she hesitates to say to the whole community what she feels about patient behavior, fearing consciously or unconsciously that some of her prejudices or tendency to have favorites may become apparent to all. Moreover, her authority may be questioned by some of her aides, who may point out the irrationality or inconsistency of some of her decisions. On the other

[4]Harry Wilmer, *Social Psychiatry in Action* (Springfield, Ill., Charles C. Thomas, 1958).

hand, the aides may well feel incapable of communicating in public, fearing ridicule or possibly even later reprisals from their own senior staff.

Perhaps most important, this kind of situation calls for a more responsible role on the part of the nursing staff than they have been used to playing. In this context, the aide may talk frequently about her desire for further education and speak resentfully about the poor quality of the in-service training, if any, but the other side of the coin is that frequently she is afraid of change. In fact, she may prefer the passive-dependent role that gives her the relative absence of responsibility, and, of course, an opportunity to grumble quite legitimately about her devalued position. The important point is that no community meeting is likely to be very effective until such time as the unit personnel really believe that it has value, not only for the patients but for themselves.

Clearly the nature of the patient population is extremely important. In a busy admission unit with a rapid turnover of patients, it is difficult to get any continuity of culture. Some patients may begin to appreciate daily meetings just when they have to leave. Many more will probably never see anything useful in this for them before they leave the ward to return home or are transferred to one of the long-stay wards. My experience would indicate that one really needs at least a nucleus of moderately long-stay patients to help the newer patients perceive the community meeting as a place where they can, from the start, expect to get an answer to some of their difficulties and/or insight into their own behavior. Daily community meetings will tend to produce in both patients and staff an increasing awareness of the nature and predisposing factors behind disturbed behavior. This in turn tends to produce changes in the social structure of the ward so that further disturbances can be, in part, prevented, and better handled when they occur. It may become clear that patients leave the handling of "incidents" entirely to the nursing staff. At the same time, the nursing staff may be criticized for their actions in these incidents, some patients feeling that they have been too perfunctory or too rough or have used restraints when they were not necessary, and so on.

In such a discussion, the likelihood is that many of the patients will bring forward factors about the incident that change its significance for all concerned. They often see where the patient's behavior had been misunderstood by the staff, and the tendency is for the patients slowly to become more responsible in relation to the handling and even restraint of their peers. Thus, the passive-dependent attitude, which is so often associated with the role of the patient, comes to be modified in the direction of more active participation in relation to acting out behavior or other incidents, and becomes much more closely identified with the staff role. Another example of this is the way in which the patients and staff respond to a patient leaving the community meeting. In many instances, the incident passes apparently unnoticed, but if the doctor or other staff member begins to draw attention to the fact that so-and-so leaves at some significant point and suggests that the departure has something to do with the patient's anxiety, then the unit personnel tends to become more sensitive to the meaning of behavior. In time, the patients will probably come to talk about doing something to bring the anxious member back into the community meeting where his anxiety can be examined.

A sharing of responsibility for patient behavior is particularly important in relation to the night staff. Unfortunately, they are frequently the ones who are not present at community meetings or the discussions that should, in my opinion, always follow a community meeting. Communication to them must be through the morning or evening shifts, with overlap. The evening staff tends to be isolated from the morning teaching programs. The interest of the evening and night shifts can be aroused most effectively by the duty doctor explaining the significance of community meetings and telling them how much any written or verbal feedback that they care to offer is appreciated. However, their anxieties about the day staff and their lack of familiarity with the treatment culture may make this difficult. Also, being left alone on the ward with patients about whom they may know very little and who may cause them considerable anxiety, often makes them feel that their point of view might be distorted or misunderstood if it is handled by people other than themselves. In rare instances, the night staff or evening shift may be so interested that they choose to stay on or arrive early to participate in the ward community meeting in which case their difficulties can be expressed directly to the patients and staff. Fort Logan Mental Health Center, Denver, has avoided this difficulty in part, because nurses (R.N.s, mental health workers, technicians, etc.) rotate through the three shifts and never become isolated from the system as would be the case otherwise.

Patient councils are popular and found in many hospital organizations. The function of these ward councils varies considerably, but in the main, in my experience, they are limited to the handling of practical ward details, such as privileges, arrangements for ward cleaning, rosters, and so on. Nevertheless, they tend through time to assume increasing responsibilities. In my opinion, patient councils should not assume too much responsibility unaided and should be supervised by staff, and the content of the discussions in their council meetings should be fed back to the community meetings. It seems to me that much good can come from the development of patient responsibility that is skillfully supervised. Nevertheless, it would be foolish to assume that this kind of development occurs without considerable conflict.

If the patient council is allowed to develop responsibilities without having staff to turn to in times of need, and without an adequate feedback of their council meetings, it is more than likely that they will find themselves isolated and resented by their peers. They may come to assume all the characteristics of authority figures and much of the hostility that was previously directed toward the staff will be shifted toward them. It is for reasons like this that I feel that the staff should be present at council meetings, and when necessary, should point out what is happening. A staff member might feel a need to point out that certain decisions ought to be fed through the patient community as a whole before being finalized by the council. If the council does not feed back its deliberations and difficulties to the community meeting, there is a danger that its role may become misunderstood; thus, the council's peers may come to feel that the council is no longer made up of members of the patient group, but rather of people who are ganging up with the staff and are in some kind of alien authoritative relationship with the patients.

In my experience, the council, and particularly the chairman, may find this difficulty so real that deterioration in his clinical condition may occur. In general, one could say that through time, the staff responsibilities can be transferred in part to the patient population and particularly to the patient council with real benefit in creating a more varied and responsible role for the patients. At the same time, the general principle could be formulated that the degree of responsibility that the patients can usefully assume is inversely related to the degree of disorganization within a ward. Thus, at times of relatively satisfactory organization, with appropriate leaders within the patient population and free communications, the amount of responsibility that can be safely transferred to the patients is maximal, whereas in times of disorganization, when the group ego, if one likes to use the term, is weak, then the staff must assume increasing responsibility for decision making and the general direction of patient management.[5]

The Staff Review

With the increasing interest in the social environment of the patient, the role of the ward psychiatrist and of other team members becomes more complex. It is not enough to be a competent diagnostician and individual therapist; the team members must also learn how to recognize and modify the social organization and culture of the ward, as well as the complexities of group treatment.

This can best be accomplished by a daily community meeting, as already described, which lasts about an hour, immediately followed by a review involving all staff members. This affords an opportunity to examine the response of the various personnel with different skills, expectations, and prejudices, who have been exposed to the same interactional scene in the community meeting. I find that for training purposes, a staff meeting or a review of this kind should last for about an hour. In this setting, it is possible to discuss the perceptions and feelings of the staff retrospectively in relation to the community meeting and to examine their interaction during the staff meeting.

Let us assume that all staff who come in contact with the patient in a therapeutic role will be present at both meetings. In the review they will, in varying degrees, be able to express both their analysis of certain aspects of the community meeting and their feelings. If we take a frequently recurring problem, such as authority, the aides may perceive this in terms of their own desire to conform to a strict authority system in which implementation of the re-

[5]Seymour Parker, "Disorganization in a Psychiatric Ward," *Psychiatry* 22 (1959):65–168.

quirements of higher authority are of prime importance. The cleanliness of the ward, the observation of smoking rules, and the avoidance of incidents are necessary if they are to avoid undue anxiety. In this context, they will tend to express, directly and indirectly, views that support the maintenance of patient discipline. At the other extreme, the doctors, if they have had considerable training and experience in examining the social interaction in a ward, may perceive untidiness or dirt in the ward as symptoms of disorganization among the patients and want to examine this as a form of communication. To do this at all skillfully, the anxieties of the aides will have to be given due consideration, and the realities of their position faced frankly.

In discussion, it may emerge that the aides are uncomfortable at community meetings, feel that the meetings take up far too much of their time, and are responsible in part for the untidiness of the ward. They may point out that continued disapproval from higher authorities may result in possible loss of employment. The reality of this fear may be reinforced by the fact that their supervisors are themselves not trained in social psychiatry and may apply a value system to their area of responsibility that is at variance with the developing culture in the unit. It may be that a long-term plan involving training seminars with the supervisors will be a necessary adjunct to the effective functioning of the unit if the situation is to be rendered therapeutic. At the same time, it may appear that the anxiety of the aides stems in part from their personality difficulties, attributable to their relatively inadequate education and lack of sophistication, which hampers them in their role relationship with more highly trained personnel. They may deal with this by denial and rationalization, blaming the frequency of community meetings and lack of discipline for the unsatisfactory state of affairs. A situation of this kind is not infrequent and the mere gain in insight on the part of an aide may not in itself be enough. It may take a long period of education and support to tide them over the transition from their previous image of a structured, simplified role to that of a therapeutic one.

What has been said about the role of the aide in a ward problem bearing on authority applies in different ways to all the roles and role-relationships within the unit.

The charge nurse may have particular difficulties in that, by contrast with the aide, she has a relatively higher status and a professional image that implies knowledge, which frequently she does not possess. In the United States, she may have had no formal training in psychiatry other than a short affiliation as a student nurse. Most R.N.s have been trained in a fairly strict, authoritarian culture and have little experience in the examination of roles and role relationships, the sharing of responsibility, and the concept of group decisions or group treatment. She may resent both the loss of her relatively exclusive relationship with the doctor and the staff's examination of her handling of patients' problems. In the review, it may become clear that when she feels threatened by patients, she resorts to devices such as recommending shock treatment, transferring the patient to another ward, or regressing to an authoritarian disciplinary role. Like the aide, she too has the problem of a nursing authority structure. She is expected to satisfy the needs of personnel who have no direct contact with the ward and who view things from their own particular nursing perspective. Unless nursing supervisors and the higher echelons of nursing can themselves become identified with community treatment programs, then confusion of roles is almost inevitable. The ward views the problems as material for treatment, whereas the nursing hierarchy tends to view them as administrative problems calling for immediate action. One device frequently used by the nursing profession is to transfer a nurse to another ward if there are repeated ward problems. By doing this, of course, nothing is learned from the disturbance on the ward, but, from the point of view of administration, the problem is eliminated.

Nurses from the department of education may, with advantage, also be involved in this kind of learning experience. If they have student nurses on a ward, they tend to teach them in a situation that is removed from the actual ward interaction. If, however, the nursing education personnel themselves become involved in community meetings and find a functional role in the ward, they are then in a position to discuss the interactional scene with their students in the staff review and in their own teaching seminars. In this way, their own perceptions of what went on and what they would normally teach their students can be examined by other trained personnel, and nursing education puts itself in the position of having a continuous education experience instead of tending to become stereotyped.

Moreover, the staff review is an ideal setting in which to work through some of the problems inherent in the role relationships between medical, nursing service, and nursing education personnel. All three have a significant relationship with the student nurse, and unless a serious attempt is made to work through this relationship, the student may find herself confused, and at times, victimized. What she wants above all is someone to turn to when she is in emotional difficulties with her patients. My feeling is that in the kind of program we are discussing, she will be able to turn to the charge nurse, to the nursing education supervisor, or to the ward personnel, including the doctor, social worker, psychologist, and so on, all of whom should be in a position to understand certain aspects of the problems of nurse-patient relationships on the ward. This implies a degree of sophistication of all ward personnel, which tends to evolve over a period of time through daily staff meetings when the problems of treatment, ward management, interpersonal relationships, including staff relationships, are under constant scrutiny and discussion.

What we have said about the roles of the personnel in direct contact with the patient applies equally to the more peripheral roles, including the social worker and psychologist. It seems to me that it is equally important that their relationships with patients, whether as social case workers or as therapists or group workers, should be discussed freely with the total unit staff personnel. This implies that roles are constantly being modified and that a psychologist or social worker in Unit A need not necessarily have a similar role in Unit B. In fact, it seems a pity if professional personnel become identified with their own professional subgroup rather than with the unit in which they are working. All this implies a considerable degree of skill and sophistication on the part of the unit leader, who at the present time, is usually the psychiatrist.[6] There seems to me no adequate reason this responsibility should continue to rest with the psychiatrist unless he has the kind of training and skill that we are discussing. This leadership role could reasonably be given to one of the other staff personnel, provided, of course, that the purely medical matters were left, as they must be, to the doctor.

In order to become competent in handling the various role relationships and management problems that we have been discussing, the team leader is forced to attempt to examine the problems of the various personnel and see them from not only his own but from other points of view. Whether group consensus can be seen as a satisfactory way of resolving problems, if indeed it is ever achieved, is an open question, but the attempt to examine problems in various dimensions is a rich learning experience. Obviously, it is much better if this whole procedure is supervised by a social scientist with experience in psychiatry or by a mental health professional who has had considerable expe-

[6]At Fort Logan Mental Health Center, Denver, Colorado, the majority of the team leaders are not psychiatrists, but belong to other disciplines.

rience in group work and the social science field. Such training will help him to make optimal use of his staff and the social environment generally, and where psychiatrists are concerned, will be invaluable preparation for a possible future role as a mental health administrator.

Peer Group Potential for Change (Health)

If one assumes that the patient population has certain treatment potentials that can be developed under constant medical and other professional supervision, then one has to set up a structure whereby the patient contribution can be maximized. The immediate objection can be raised that the patients are ill and it is unfair or unrealistic to expect them to help in treatment and make decisions involving a good deal of responsibility; in any case, this is the job that the staff is paid to do. On the other hand, it can be argued that perhaps the most outstanding characteristic of newly admitted patients is their feeling of depression and despair, and if possible, they must be helped to deal with this. A former colleague, Gil Elles, a psychoanalyst working at the therapeutic community at Henderson Hospital, London (formerly the Social Rehabilitation Unit at Belmont Hospital), described the handling of this problem as follows.

> The community has developed techniques for dealing with this problem at a conscious level, and at the same time has become aware of the unconscious mechanisms which are all the time operating to prevent individual, group, or community from becoming overwhelmed by this despair. In the first instance emphasis is placed on trying to lessen the force of unconscious guilt which drives the patient compulsively into trouble again and again, and seriously inhibits his capacity to learn by experience. With the new patient this takes the form of making known to the community his problem so that the earliest possible moment in treatment he is accepted for what he *is* rather than what he would *like* to be, or what he

fears himself to be. In this way, it is hoped that the deep-seated guilt is somewhat diminished and the patient's ego strengths are increased and made more available to him.

In the second place every patient has a dual role both of trying to accept and give treatment. Therefore, through the second part of his role his self-regard is fortified enabling him to feel less of a failure because he is expected to help and understand others. Thus, in the long run he is able to feel less threatened in admitting some part of his own desperation about himself.

In the third instance and following on from these initial community attitudes, despair is limited by improving communication within the individual and between individuals in their various groups. The community has a culture whereby feelings are shared very openly and the reasons for such feelings examined in great detail. To do this the day has to be geared so that every community activity is associated with a long period for discussion about it. Furthermore, the various activity groups are so interrelated that the maximum contact in as many social roles as possible is provided for each patient in the community. In effect this experience tends to build up in each individual a more integrated picture of himself, firstly as seen by others, and finally when accepted by him as part of his own self-evaluation.

What has happened in such situations following admission is that a reduction of the violence and fragmentation of the individual splitting processes has taken place. This means that the despairing patient's urgent need to project wholesale the unacceptable parts of himself—good as well as bad—has been diminished in the first place by the community's attitude of understanding and acceptance. This enables the patient to be aware of new strength so long as he remains a member of the community. By establishing firm bonds through patient-staff and patient-patient interaction which all the while is looked at and discussed, a framework is then secondarily built up that is strong enough to carry the weight of a personal depression of a more mature order. Thus, some patients for the first time experience both another security and an inner despair which allows them to feel and to understand the emotions of remorse and pity, followed by a longing for and a belief in their own ability to repair and restore the fabric of damaged relationships. For

> such a patient this means that authority figures are gradually perceived as less threatening and other relationships as more lasting. Thus, the patient in internalizing a conscience now less punitive can accept both more responsibility and more success.[7]

This principle of elaborating the role of a patient to one of therapist is, I think, one of the fundamental tenets of community treatment procedure. This concept is often mistakenly seen as handing over ultimate responsibility to the patients. This, in my opinion, is not practicable and what one wishes to do is to give the patients the optimal responsibility compatible with their overall capacity at any one time, and in no sense does the staff or the doctor in charge relinquish his ultimate authority, which merely remains latent to be invoked when necessary. It is the application of this principle which calls for considerable experience and skill. As an example, a community may be functioning at a fairly high level of effectiveness and the patients may be able to take over a considerable amount of responsibility, and then, on a particular day, four or five of the most responsible and successfully treated members leave to be replaced by four or five new patients, who may be in the state of considerable disorganization.

The loss of patient leadership within the ward and the effect of the new intake may be such that the ward functioning is materially altered and the staff may have to play a much more active and controlling role than they had been previously doing.[8] This is not fundamentally different from what happens in an individual or a group treatment session when the lack of ego strength or anxiety level is such that the therapist feels it necessary to be largely supportive for

[7]Gil Elles, "Research into the Aftercare Needs of Discharged Patients," 1961, unpublished paper. Henderson Hospital, London.

[8]Parker, "Disorganization on a Psychiatric Ward," p. 65.

a time. We are talking about patient responsibility of a higher order than one usually understands by the term patient government. Patient government is usually restricted to decisions on relatively minor matters of ward organization and activities. What we have in mind is decisions shared with the staff and involving such matters as the discharge of patients or transfer to other wards or what disciplinary action should be taken in the case of deviant behavior. This sharing of serious responsibility with the staff is, I think, one of the most important ways of overcoming the lack of confidence, low self-estimate, and overdependency, which all too frequently is characteristic of the psychiatric patient in the hospital ward. This responsibility can also be carried over to the patient's work roles.[9]

It is ideal if one can do production work for the community and have patient foremen, timekeepers, etc. If one is fortunate enough to have the freedom to build up a therapeutic community from the point of view of the patients' social and treatment needs, then one must inevitably end up with a structure that deviates markedly from the more usual pattern in which the organization is essentially staff centered and often is determined by traditions from the past, which have little relevance to current treatment methods and practices. As an example, one finds that a ward in which the patients have a great deal of identification with responsible roles and with treatment, they will come to the aid of the night nurse in the event of disturbed patient behavior instead of leaving it entirely for the staff to deal with. In this context also, the patients come to feel much more able to bear with highly disturbed behavior among their peers because the community meetings help

[9]Maxwell Jones, "Social Rehabilitation with Emphasis on Work Therapy As a Form of Group Therapy," *British Journal of Medical Psychology* 33 (1960): 67–71.

them to understand the meaning of the disturbed behavior and gives them a better idea of how to relate in a helpful and understanding way to the sick member.

The daily examination of behavior and current problems means that the patients become aware of the factors that lie behind behavior and learn a great deal about each other's problems. In any type of hospital, they are forced to relate to other patients and staff at ward level whether they like it or not, and it seems reasonable to try to help them to have a positive role to play and a much better insight into what is going on in themselves and in those around them. In my experience, it is possible to get patients and staff at all levels to appreciate some of the phenomena that occur on the unit and in the daily community meetings. The process that occurs in these meetings through time has much in common with ordinary group treatment. In the first instance, the patients in the community meeting tend to look to the staff for leadership and are glad when some general topic is raised that has no personal significance. As time progresses, they begin to talk about some of their deeper feelings and to test the staff reactions to them. Assuming adequate skills on the part of the staff, they become used as transference figures to the advantage of the treatment process. The same applies to the transference onto various members of the patient population.

The concepts of manifest and latent content, the unconscious, and ego defenses come to be understood in much the way that occurs in a small group. It may be necessary to have additional seminars for the aides who are less well trained than the other staff members and for whom the change of role implicit in this discussion is greater than that required of any other staff member. For the staff review, concepts like feedback from informal staff-patient groups and difficulties occurring during the night between patients and night staff can be usefully communicated to the group. Ideally, of course, one would hope that nursing personnel rotate so that the night staff has an opportunity to participate in the learning experience afforded to the day staff, more particularly the morning shift.

The meetings described are clearly less specifically therapeutic and more concerned with everyday behavior and ward management than is the typical therapeutic group of six or eight patients of a selected kind. Nevertheless, community meetings of up to 50 patients and staff have a particular place in institutional therapy, particularly in bringing about the establishment of what one might call a therapeutic culture. By this is meant that the day-after-day examination of the problems existing in a ward and the consideration of the roles of all staff members and of the patients leads, through time, to considerable modification of the ward structure. Not only that, but the traditional attitudes and beliefs can come under scrutiny, and we then are in a position to ask ourselves why we do what we do when we do it. A learning experience of this kind is far from easy and clearly causes the staff considerable anxiety.

In the foregoing account of a therapeutic community I have used the word treatment frequently. I have come to prefer the more generic term social learning.

Treatment suggests a doctor doing something to a passive recipient (the patient). Admittedly, such a concept is modified in psychiatry where the interaction between doctor and patient has a dynamic quality largely lacking in general medicine. This opening up of the system is carried even further by group psychotherapy where the doctor studiously avoids being manipulated into the role of teacher and tries to get the group to interact among themselves, while he acts as a trained (group dynamics) resource person. The motivation of the group is determined by their need and desire to get well. This dimension varies greatly from person to person, and for many people illness provides secondary gains that may be outside consciousness and block any real motivation to change. The group leader may be a psychiatrist or other professional with training in group psychotherapy. Even a psychoanalytic training will not ensure any standardization of group methods. Each group psychotherapist tends to be a law unto himself and his methods will reflect his own personality, beliefs, and values, as well as his formal training.

The mental health professional in the role of group psychotherapist or family therapist is facilitating change, but his primary focus is on some aspect of health. The facilitator (process consultant or interventionist) in other systems, e.g., industry or schools, is primarily concerned with the functioning of the system. The distinction becomes somewhat arbitrary when a family is being seen as a system rather than a collection of disturbed individuals, one or more of whom have identified symptoms.

If psychiatry plans to widen its commitments to include social problem areas in society at large, family therapy and community psychiatry would seem to offer a possible link. But no one is too clear about the term community psychiatry. If it is to include training and experience with problems other than mental health, then we must include systems theory, communication theory, and learning theory in our basic training, together with a much greater exposure than exists at present to the behavioral sciences. This metamorphosis may be at the expense of a further subdivision of specialty in psychiatry, i.e., social psychiatry or social ecology. Unless this new emphasis is developed, it may be that psychiatry will be limited to the "case" and may be involved in social problem areas only in relation to identifiable "illness."

It has already been suggested that family and group treatment comes very close to the behavioral scientist's concept of systems change. Where psychiatrists talk of treatment, the behavioral scientists tend to talk about organization development, learning, or growth. The term social learning[10] has been used in many ways. By this term I mean two-way communication motivated by some inner need or stress leading to the overt or covert expression of feeling and involving cognitive processes and change. Such learning may relate to the individual, group, or system. Psychoanalysis and ego psychology have added a great deal to our knowledge of learning and the therapeutic process, which are intimately linked. Freud described thinking as a substitute for acting, that is, acting in fantasy. Tension, resulting from innate need or unresolved problems, supplies the motive driving force to resolve the situation, either by trial and error or by some cognitive process. When a solution has been achieved, a feeling of satisfaction ensues. In this sense, the therapeutic process can be described in terms of learning theory. To quote from Alexander:

> During treatment the patient unlearns old patterns and learns new ones. This complex process of relearning follows the same principles as the more simple relearning processes hitherto studied by experimental psychologists. It contains cognitive elements as well as learning from actual interpersonal experiences which occur during the therapeutic interaction. These two components are intricately interwoven. They are described in psychoanalytical literature with the undefined, rather vague term "emotional insight." The word "emotional" refers to the interpersonal experiences; the word "insight" refers to the cognitive element. The expression does not mean more than the recognition of the presence of both components. The psychological process to which the term refers is not yet spelled out in detail.[11]

The introduction of the feeling level in interpersonal exchange introduces a crucial element in social learning.

[10]Jones, *Beyond the Therapeutic Community.*

[11]Franz Alexander, "The Dynamics of Psychotherapy in the Light of Learning Theory," *American Journal of Psychiatry* 120 (1963): 440.

Western culture frowns on the free expression of feeling and superimposes values such as politeness, good taste, and morality, which tend to obscure the individual's feelings. Conformity to the mores and expectations of society is a very powerful element in our educational and family systems. To deny to such an extent the free expression of feeling is to limit the opportunity for social learning.

It is essential that we add to the conscious aspect of feeling the concept of corrective emotional experience: over a period of time emotionally charged attitudes developed in childhood have to be corrected by reliving similar situations in the immediate present.[12] One important factor in bringing about change and learning is that the teacher—or psychoanalyst—behaves very differently in the present situation, compared with the parents in the past. As an example, the child of a dominant parent may be forced to repress his own rebellious, aggressive responses in order to avoid the parent's anger. Such timidity may persist into adult life and can only be modified when a tolerant and understanding teacher—or therapist—behaves very differently in situations in which the individual anticipates anger or rejection. In a therapeutic community there are many opportunities in the ordinary life of the patient—or trainee—in which neurotic patterns of timidity, fear, and so on, which are derived from the past, can be reproduced in the present and handled much more effectively in the presence of an understanding and therapeutically skilled authority figure. In brief, social learning includes both conscious and unconscious elements, although the use made of the latter depends largely on the training and experience of the individual teacher or therapist.

It seems to me that social learning describes the function of the facilitator (process consultant or intervention-

[12]F. Alexander and T. M. French, *Psychoanalytic Therapy: Principles and Application* (New York: Ronald Press, 1946).

ist), whether he be operating in a treatment situation or helping an industrial or other system. In other words, I am suggesting that if psychiatry is to include social problem areas outside "illness," then a semantic modification might avoid confusion. Social learning would represent a more all-embracing term than treatment, and the term facilitator has a wider meaning than the word therapist. By the same token, positive outcomes in psychotherapy might be expressed in terms of change or growth rather than "cure" in much the same way as in an effective change from a closed to an open system.

But will the sacred cow of treatment, the hallmark of the doctor's uniqueness in society, give way to such more generalized concepts as social learning and growth? Anyone with hospital experience knows that in the past anything a doctor does to a patient tends to be dignified by the term treatment. Interaction with the other helping professions—nurses, social workers, etc.—has less prestige for the patient. The fact is that most ordinary individuals want very badly to live, and to reassure themselves, they are only too ready to project onto doctors an aura of magic. The medical profession, with notable exceptions, is not averse to reinforcing such an illusion. In such an atmosphere, collusion is common; the patient refrains from asking the doctor embarrassing questions that might expose areas of ignorance; similarly the doctor spares the patient by not dwelling on the unknowns regarding diagnosis, prognosis, etc. Admittedly there are positive elements in such collusion, such as sparing the patient or his relatives unnecessary suffering, but in the relatively closed systems that most hospitals represent, there is little opportunity for open communication and learning.

I am suggesting that the mystique of medicine may result in resistance to change in the direction of an open system with the same intensity as other systems like industry, schools, or colleges.

The remedy as I see it, would be to expose the medical student to an open system during his undergraduate years. Our experience of medical students is that they tend to be overworked and immersed in memorizing facts, and preoccupied with future exams. They feel dehumanized and have little identity as individuals. They survive somehow and have a vague belief that when they become M.D.s things will change for the better. Those who escape into private practice are inevitably exposed to real life experiences and may become effective as a result of some form of social learning. Those who remain in hospitals, in teaching, research, or service posts, inevitably tend to perpetuate the closed system that is medicine. No one has the time or the inclination to look at the system as it affects the consumer (or the staff). A facilitator in such a system has a problem regarding motivation to change.

I have drawn an extreme picture to illustrate the point that medicine, like other professions and occupations, has certain attitudes and values by which it is identified. The resistance to change may come both from the operator and the consumer, e.g., the public's hope that the medical profession can keep them alive indefinitely. To meet such expectations and avoid open communication may help to perpetuate the status quo.

Happily the climate in many medical schools is changing. The following section is quoted from a report (unpublished) on medical curriculum written by four medical students: Curtis Canning, Davis Christensen, James Emery, and David Green, at the end of their four years of undergraduate studies at the University of Utah (May, 1973).

The Learning Environment

> Medicine is a proliferating field in which considerable advances in knowledge are being made each year. The amount of essential scientific material that the student must assimi-

late and understand in order to practice competent medicine increases in direct proportion to the number of such advances. If medicine is to continue to train adequate practitioners in the face of this expansion, medical curricula must strive to frequently redefine and expand the core of knowledge that each physician must have, and must also attempt to find new methods to enable the student to learn more effectively and more efficiently. What is known about the dynamic process of learning implies certain methods of instruction or modes of learning. And the learning environment provides the surroundings in which these methods can be applied or utilized. Both have been neglected in the planning of medical curricula.

Learning is a complex activity with different levels of cognitive sophistication. The most advanced and complex level is that of problem solving, which requires utilization of other intellectual skills such as the ability to associate, to generalize and to discriminate (concept learning) and the ability to abstract, to infer or predict and to test (rule learning).[13]

The acquisition of these cognitive skills has definite curricular implications. Concept learning as observed in children results quite naturally from trial and error type behavior or inquiry. Certainly medical school should not inhibit a basic experimental, trial and error approach to learning. Expecially in the early stages of his experience, the medical student should be allowed to learn from failure. Concept learning is aided by precise descrimination between the defining and nondefining attributes (or concrete references) as well as by repetition of that discrimination process.[14] The lecture technique is not incompatible with this aspect of concept formation. However, personally initiated trial and error type inquiry must be a concomitant learning activity. That is, the learner must be an *active* participant.

Rule learning involves the recognition of relationships between concepts.These key relationships facilitate the development of skills in predicting and testing and allow one to establish behavior strategies. Problem solving involves behavior based on learned strategies and predictive skills at

[13]Robert M. Gagné, *The Conditions of Learning* (New York: Holt Rinehart and Winston, 1970), pp. 214–216.

[14]Gagné, Ibid.

the cognitive level as well as on various motor skills. Gagné maintains that what makes problem solving different from elaborate rule learning is some factor(s) "within the learner."[15] Perhaps, in part, he alludes to motivation when he says, "The solving of a problem may be guided by a greater or lesser amount of verbal communication supplied from the outside, but the most essential variables are internal ones. . . . When problem solution is achieved, something is also *learned,* in the sense that the individual's capability is more or less permanently changed. What emerges . . . is a *higher-order* rule, which thereupon becomes a part of the individual's repertory."[16]

With these things in mind, a learning environment should challenge the student whenever possible in a problem-solving way (as opposed to a method emphasizing rote recall, for example). Most of the problems should be real and active; when this is impossible, simulation of actual problems (preferably clinically directed) should be utilized.

Perhaps more than any other field, medicine requires continual self-learning and improvement to maintain competency. If the right attitude toward learning is not developed, then in a sense no matter how much fact is taught medical education has failed. The desire or lack of desire for continual self-learning once out of the college environment is, in part, a function of the environment and attitudes which characterized the student's training. If the student has had a disagreeable experience with formal education, he is less likely to return to an environment which reminds him of that distasteful experience—even if he could improve himself by doing so. To some degree this fact is manifested by the hesitancy of many medical students to pursue further work in the basic sciences, largely as a result of distasteful experiences during the freshman and sophomore years. The close, perhaps subconscious association of learning with tedium or unpleasant work is also demonstrated by faculty and administrators who feel students must be forced to learn, that without constant external constraint learning will not occur.

[15]Gagné, Ibid.
[16]Gagné, Ibid.

Chapter 7

ACTION MODELS FOR CHANGE (OPEN SYSTEM)

I would now like to consider the problem of change toward an open system in three different mental health facilities presenting quite different social systems: (a) a medical school with a psychiatric department concerned with training and treating approximately 100 inpatients from a population of approximately 400,000, (b) a state hospital in an area of approximately 500,000, with 800 to 900 inpatients at any one time, (c) a community mental health center.

In the first two cases, I acted as a consultant for two weeks with the specific assignment to apply a systems approach to the facility and recommend and effect, if possible, changes in the direction of an open system. In the last example, I spent eighteen months as a facilitator or process consultant one day a week.

A Psychiatric Unit In a Medical School

The System

The first-year residents in psychiatry spent the whole year in the inpatient service. They were carefully supervised by several experienced (attending) psychiatrists as well as by the head of the residency program and a senior (third-year) resident who acted as team leader on the ward. By good fortune rather than planning, one of the first-year residents, Iris Asher, M.D., with help from two other first-year residents had been keeping notes of my interaction with her ward. I was unaware of this at the time, but gaining this information near the end of my stay, asked if they would continue keeping a record after my departure. To this they agreed, but unfortunately their program meant that they would leave the ward in three months time to start their second year of residency training. The following description is quoted from their report.

> Maxwell Jones spent two weeks working on a traditional inpatient service at a large city hospital in the role of consultant or in his terminology as "facilitator" for "social learning." The ward staff considered themselves to be working in a therapeutic community. Staff consisted of a head nurse, nurses, nursing aides, a chief resident, first-year residents, medical students, a psychology intern, a social work supervisor and family therapist, social work students, a rehabilitation student, an activities therapist, a ward attending, and a consultant in family and group process.
>
> The theoretical basis for such an undertaking stems from a growing movement to apply some socio-theoretical frame of reference in addition to a psycho-theoretical one to a clinical situation which is largely phenomenologically social.
>
> Max Jones was introduced into a ward system that had been working together for eight months. The first meeting was recorded one month prior to arranging for his consultation. Then follows a section describing the actual process as

it evolved with the facilitator present. The final section illustrates selections of the process as it continued during the two weeks following his depature.

Data

In an effort to illustrate some of the lines of tension which had developed among staff in our therapeutic community, a meeting occurring one month before Max Jones' arrival is described. Approximately two weeks prior to this meeting, a 26-year old agitated schizophrenic woman, J.P., had been admitted to the ward and had physically assaulted two nurses and consequently had spent a substantial amount of time in the "seclusion room."

The meeting is held to discuss the ward management of difficult patients. The head nurse begins by describing the aggressive acting out behavior of J.P. and the frequency with which the nurses have had to resort to using the seclusion room in dealing with the threat of physical harm. Almost immediately, a medical student, a newcomer on the ward, focuses on an area of conflict by pointing out that in spite of his inexperience on the ward, the "cold" and "inhumane" seclusion room arouses strong feelings in him. He begins to question the necessity and utility of secluding the patient. The topic is not a new one and staff takes their usual positions on either side of the issue. Nursing led by the head nurse argues the absolute necessity of the practice in the light of the limited staff/patient ratio, absence of male attendants, and the usual presence of more than one potentially violent patient on the ward at any one time. The ward attending (a psychiatrist) jumps in to support the nurses and states that many patients profit therapeutically from the seclusion room and even thank the staff later for imposing control. Both ward attending and nursing staff are members of permanent ward staff. In contrast, on the other side of the issue, the transient ward staff, residents, medical students, and activity workers, speak heatedly. The activities therapist recalls that earlier in the year when seclusion was questioned as a punitive measure, the nurses avoided the issue. The resident makes the point that we must be willing to learn by considering the ideal treatment setting and not declare a practice desirable because it is utilitarian. The medical student feels that staff protection should not justify treatment reminiscent of a "repressive jail." The consultant in group process attempts conciliation by stressing human limitations among staff who can only tolerate so much abuse. The chief resident is noticeably silent in the discussion, although he is clearly the main authority figure on the ward. A confrontation has developed, feelings are high and formerly held positions colored by hidden resentments are surfacing. Staff is splitting along lines of permanent versus transient.

The meeting then climaxes in a rapid series of poorly understood events. Without explanation the head nurse, the main proponent of the use of seclusion, leaves the room. In an effort to continue the discussion the ward attending becomes more and more exasperated and also walks out. Disorganization and confusion hold sway. A medical student goes out to speak with the head nurse and ward attending and returns to say that both parties have refused to return and continue the discussion. Inside the meeting most staff members want to believe that the attending's exit was unrelated to the highly emotional nature of the meeting, others argue that it is. In this state of uncertainty, the chief closes the meeting stating that the level of feelings is "out of hand" and that we can discuss the subject at a later date.

The meeting closes, stressful silences and whispered conversations characterize the subsequent days.

In the observations of the staff meetings which follow Max Jones' arrival, the methodology of the facilitator emerges. In the first meeting held on the ward with Max as the facilitator, the nursing staff is unable to attend and Max wants to know why, thereby identifying a problem. The head nurse is asked and she explains the staff shortage problem: there is only one nurse to watch the floor. Max has begun his method, identifying a problem and supporting the lower members of the hierarchy, the nurses. The effect of this action is that the following day at our meeting with Max all of the nurses are available. Did the nursing shortage disappear overnight?

In fact, the nurses from our ward arranged for coverage by staff from another ward. The support offered interested them and they wanted to know more. In our second meeting with most of the staff from various disciplines present (nurses, doctors, social service, activities) the stage was set for the facilitator. What does he do? He begins to question the system, specifically the medical model, whereby the doctors are the chief decision makers. The staff begins to complain: the nurses about being offered treatment responsibility for the patient that no one is interested in; the activities therapist about his lack of status on the ward; the residents about the authoritarian attitude of the chief. What has happened? Max has encouraged confrontation by encouraging the confronters. He uses the term risk takers and applies it in one instance to the activities therapist when he confronts the chief resident, or in another to the social work supervisor when she complains about the chief's lack of support. In this meeting a lot of grumbling is focused on the chief: he is too controlling, too rigid, too authoritarian. What does the facilitator do now? He begins to support the chief resident by saying that he, Max, thinks that the chief is really open to change and willing to learn. He confronts the rest of the staff with their responsibility in helping the chief to be less controlling. The result is that the chief is not pushed out of the system and is encouraged to listen to his staff while his staff is encouraged to talk to him. Confrontation has occurred but communication is not closed off because the facilitator supports both the confronter as risk taker and the confronted as open to change.

At the end of the first week with Max on the ward, our usual Friday morning rounds turn into something other than usual. The staff meeting begins with a discussion of a patient who had been abruptly discharged by the psychology intern the evening before. The discharge had taken place without discussing it with general staff. Max asks how decisions are made. As discussion ensues it appears that although staff talks about consensus, many treatment decisions are unilateral ones. Staff begins to discuss the issue. Risk takers emerge. The social work students explain why they are unwilling to assume the role of primary therapists. They consider the rest of the staff unsupportive. Confrontation and communication continue and consensus is reached on two major issues: staff will attempt to reach consensus on all major treatment decisions; and the role of the primary therapist will be open to all, instead of just the residents and psychology intern. In this meeting in addition to the positive push for change, resistance to change emerges. Both the chief resident and the ward attending want the staff to hold off any decision about who will be primary therapists. The rest of the staff want to make the decision now while the issue is hot. It seems as if impedance from the top is emerging.

The second week on the ward begins as if Max is not there. Monday morning rounds are held in the usual way. There have been no new patients admitted so the issue of who will be the primary therapist doesn't come up. At Tuesday morning rounds we have two newly admitted patients and the chief brings up the issue of who wants to treat the patients. This is the continuation of the group consensus reached last week. Max isn't present and dead silence prevails. Will the chief take on the role of facilitator? Instead he closes communication by saying he'll have to assign the patients to the residents. Max isn't there and no one has assumed his role.

That Tuesday morning instead of our usual case conference the staff meets with Max. The meeting begins with Max telling the staff he plans to meet with the heads of psychiatry and nursing to discuss systems for change. The social work supervisor takes a risk and asks him what about social service and confronts him saying he is going where the power is and he's a manipulator. The social work supervisor defines her role as family therapist and Max wants to know what others think of her role. The chief resident answers and a confrontation between the social work supervisor and chief ensues, each expressing his dissatisfaction with the other. At this point, the ward attending helps explain the problem. Last year another social worker was assigned to the ward as family therapist in addition to the one already there, and intense competition was set up and continues. This rivalry has been around all year but never before discussed in a staff meeting. Max uses this opportunity to teach. He suggests that the crisis between the two family therapists could have been used as a learning situation by open confrontation; instead it smoldered all year. Somewhere in the meeting the head of nursing gets up to leave and no one but Max asks her where she's going. The principle of support emerges. Max says we don't support one another and he wouldn't want to work on our ward. Here the facilitator challenges the group and identifies a problem. In this meeting some resistance is seen. The issue of primary therapists is brought up by a resident and the nurses complain: their position is too unstable, they can be shifted to night duty. The top of the nursing hierarchy says the nurses don't have enough time to do the traditional nursing functions as it is.

The following day at evening rounds without Max it is suggested that one of the nurse's aides who has developed a particularly good relationship with an adolescent patient become the primary therapist. The suggestion is made by the medical student who is presently treating the patient and is going off service. The aide agrees and plans are made to discuss the practical issues the following day at staff rounds.

At staff rounds Max is present. The nursing aide has come in on her day off. Another issue comes up first. The activities therapist has had a party for the patients with beer and wine agreed to by all the staff. At the last minute, administration external to the ward said no beer and wine, and the activities therapist went ahead anyway with the staff's implicit approval. He begins to express concern about possible action by the administrator. Max sits quietly and says nothing. The chief and head of nursing begin to question the activities man. It looks as if he'll be out on a limb and then the nursing supervisor confronts the rest of the staff and demands support for activities. So support is supplied and Max hasn't said a word, but his presence prevails. The chief brings up the issue of the nurse's aide doing primary treatment. There is general support and concrete details as to supervision are worked out. The chief appears to be learning.

At the end of two weeks certain principles about facilitation are apparent. The facilitator encourages confrontation and support for the confronters or risk takers, questions our ways of doing things, and identifies problems.

The question now is what will happen to these processes over the next two weeks as we continue to observe and Max leaves the ward.

On Friday morning Max has gone and we have rounds. An issue arises whether the psychology intern is tough enough to handle the new patient. The head nurse is a risk taker and brings up the issue. For the first time since the beginning of the year, discussion takes place about the suitability of a therapist. The social work supervisor supports the intern and a resident supports the head nurse. Communication continues and a resolution is reached. The intern will take the patient but will work closely with the rest of the staff. Another crisis is brewing: the census of patients is high and the nurses feel unsupported. The weekend is coming up and the head nurse feels uneasy. She takes a risk and says how can we be primary therapists when you don't listen to us? Heated discussion follows and a resolution is agreed upon: all therapists will arrange for passes for those patients whom the staff thinks can handle them.

On Monday rounds business is conducted as usual with a notable exception. The head nurse volunteers to take on a particular patient as primary therapist. Could it be that she felt support on Friday and now is willing to expand her role? The rest of the week seems to proceed as usual and there is less discussion of staff issues and more about patients. On Friday at rounds the psychology intern and nurses clash over the treatment of a patient. Someone suggests a special meeting and 15 minutes later staff reassembles with representatives from social service, nursing and medical disciplines, the first of such meetings ever called in response to a disagreement. Max's principle of using a crisis to learn is followed and people refer to him in the meeting. Discussion of mutual distrust between intern and nurses begins and neutral participants give support to both sides. Orders for medication are worked out and resolution to talk more is made. An overall good feeling prevails and the chief who arrives at the tail end of the meeting says, "It's things like this that make it fun to come to work."

Week four begins, the second week without Max. Monday round starts with a discussion about who wants to work with a newly admitted patient. No one responds and the chief balks, "You want responsibility and then you want me to make the decisions." Is the chief acting as a facilitator by identifying a problem? There is some discussion and the intern suggests that the chief throw it out to the group, but if there are no takers, he should assign the patient. Is this a step backwards? The social work student reveals that she and the resident have agreed for her to take on the role of primary therapist for a patient. People ask how come she hasn't said so earlier? Her reluctance and ambivalence seem obvious, but there is little support from others. Signs of resistance emerge as the ward attending and family consultant suggest that now that Max is gone anarchy is prevailing.

Is this a challenge to the chief to return to old ways? It is decided to have a staff conference on Max's effect on the ward.

At Tuesday rounds the head nurse suggests a special meeting with patients about a particular troublesome patient and the meeting is held. Are new leaders emerging?

The special meeting to discuss the anarchy that Max left is held. The ward attending and family consultant are confronted by a risk taker, the social work student. He suggests that the top of the hierarchy feels uncomfortable with the changes so they call it confusion. A resident agrees with the social work student. The chief emerges as a facilitator with the help of a resident. He and she support the top and encourage the social work student. The head nurse confronts the ward attending with a decision he made four months ago to delete one of the community meetings. The decision, she objects, was made in response to resident's desires with little concern for nursing. The head nurse and nursing, the residents, the social work students, and supervisor all say that they feel that the ward is changing and that's good. In this meeting there is confrontation, support, risk taking, and the possible emergence of a facilitator, the chief.

Three weeks after Max Jones leaves the ward a meeting is called to discuss ward reorganization. The staff wants to try open rounds with patients every morning and a post meeting to follow. The nursing supervisor quotes from Max's book *Social Psychiatry in Practice.* The chief resident and head nurse express their anxiety about the change. The head nurse is willing to try the change but the chief wants time to think it over. The meeting ends with plans for further discussion. Max Jones' presence lingers and change appears to be continuing on the ward.

Results and Discussion

Medical training and hospital practice have rigidly hierarchized the decision-making structure in the field. Whereas in many cases of a general medical nature such an absolute designation of authority and responsibility is necessary for the patients' survival, psychiatry, always the "half-brother" of medical science, seems especially liberated from the necessity of such restraints. Whether it be excessive guilt, need for responsibility, or ungratified strivings for power on the part of those involved, or more generally a resistance to change, a comfort in status, or a fear of exposure on the part of groups as a whole, the psychiatric power structure has clung fervently to the medical model with the doctor in command.

The meeting described at the outset of the section above was chosen from a series of meetings during difficult times on a typical, even prestigious inpatient service with an active academic program. Staff universally verbalized adherence to the principles and practice of the therapeutic community. In the meeting we see the most typical kind of confrontation develop where groups of individuals clash over conflicting values and beliefs. Sides are quickly taken, feelings are intensified by prior unresolved conflicts, the emotional intensity reaches intolerable levels, and the meeting dissolves chaotically. Communication has stopped, learning is impossible, and fuel is being fed to future fires. Such situations have been known to have deleterious effects on psychiatric patients for over 25 years, and are exactly what the therapeutic community was intended to improve. In this meeting, expression of feeling is suppressed, the presence of authority is felt in a variety of ways and risk takers await reprisal. Growth or change that cannot occur among staff, can never occur among patients.

The disgruntled staff which welcomed Max Jones to the ward was in fact eager to change. His method involved the leveling of vertical power structures by support for those low in the hierarchy. Traditional ways of operating on the ward were questioned by risk takers who received unbounded support. In Jones' terminology he is helping the staff to develop a "counterculture" to apply pressure on the resistance directed from the top of the hierarchy. In the presence of a truly neutral leader, sanctions were positive and the fears of reprisal lessened.

An important task for the neutral leader in addition to encouraging confrontation in a supportive atmosphere was to maximize the element of timing in such confrontations. In contrast to the chief resident in the old system, Jones allowed the level of feelings to reach appropriate heights to supply energy in a controlled manner to the conflicts. Instead of situations becoming chaotic, in the presence of skilled and trusted leadership, the process proceeded more coherently and more effectively toward attainment of group goals.

Not to be underestimated was the subtle redefinition introduced by Jones into conflict situations. "Trouble makers" were now "risk takers," conflict became "confrontation," weakening of power structure was translated into "shared decision making" or "consensus." Potentially negative situations are, by the new value system of the group, transformed into positive, growing learning experiences. In addition, the charismatic nature of the leader himself cannot be underestimated.

After the departure of Jones, it is apparent that the development of multiple leadership had begun. The head nurse took on a much more active role suggesting crisis meetings to deal with patient problems. The residents felt less inclined to wait for the chief to take an action; they suggested action themselves. The nursing supervisor suggested daily meetings which she offered to run, having experience in that area.

In general, it appeared that staff was much more involved in the daily activities of the ward, and this benefited patient care.

This writing contains observations for three weeks after Max's departure. Whether or not the change set into motion will continue is open to question. However, once people begin to move they usually continue; the difficult task is in getting them started.

Conclusion

In conclusion then it appears that our ward was a therapeutic community in name only, and that Max Jones' presence on the ward was able to effect change in a direction of more open communication. This push toward change continued after Jones' departure.

This account by Iris Asher and her two first-year resident colleagues fits well with my own record of events during my two week consulting visit, and offers a commentary for three weeks after my departure. I share her uncertainty as to the future prospects for a growth toward an open system on this particular ward. The major responsibility and power in the psychiatric wards of this medical school rests with the third-year residents. In the ward described, the third-year resident showed a considerable growth in his leadership skills and became quite an effective facilitator. Other leaders were beginning to emerge, social learning was becoming part of the ward culture, and the staff morale was rising. All this was affecting the role of the patients as individuals who had potential to help themselves and their peers. However, my visit coincided with the end of one year's stay on the ward for the chief resident and the three first-year residents. The ward function traditionally revolved around the training (largely psychoanalytic) of the residents. The emergence of a counterculture built round the needs of the patients and the permanent staff had little chance of surviving and growing unless there were powerful sanctions from the higher echelons of the authority structure. Medical school administrators as yet, show little tendency to support open systems, preferring to keep the power and control in their own hands, and this tendency is reflected in the practices of the "middle management," e.g., the third-year residents.

A State Hospital

My experience in the role of a facilitator for two weeks in a large state hospital contrasted sharply with the experience in the relatively circumscribed ward system just described.

Augusta State Hospital is one of two state hospitals serving the state of Maine with a population of almost one million. The contract, made with the superintendent and the head of the staff development department, stipulated that I look at the system as a whole with a view to its effectiveness in the delivery of services to the patient population. The patients, as with most state hospitals nowadays, were largely long-stay "institutionalized" individuals who needed a supportive system if they were to function even marginally.

The following account of my visit reflects feelings of "distance" which were inevitable in an analysis of a relatively large system that was not "visible" to the facilitator as in the case of a ward system in a medical school.

Report on Augusta State Hospital (ASH During a Two-Week Visit—June 11–22, 1973)

I. ADMINISTRATION. This aspect of ASH impressed me favorably. I met Bill Kearns, the commissioner of mental health, on two occasions, and he seemed to be a very imaginative and courageous person, something of an idealist. Dr. Schumacher, his assistant, largely concerned with the community mental health program, also showed a lot of openness to change. The appointment of Roy Ettlinger as superintendent at the age of 27 was a very enterprising step, and he has achieved remarkable progress in the short period of 18 months while at ASH. His program of management by objectives has set a pace, which his four unit chiefs have managed to maintain with considerable success. There is no hard data to prove that the dramatic drop in bed occupancy has been beneficial or otherwise to the patient population who have been transferred to çommunity living. Nevertheless, the hospital staff seem, almost without exception, to believe that this is a progressive step. At the same time, people admitted that it would be very desirable to have a follow-up study of say, 100 consecutive discharges to see what has happened to them. In January 1970, the hospital patient population was 1,557, and in June 1972, it had dropped to 894.

This picture of efficient management is not as clearly

reflected in the field of patient care. I was struck by the fact that most of the actual "treatment" seemed to be by groups that usually consisted of five or six patients under the care of an aide or, as the position is now called, mental health worker. Despite efforts to set up aide training programs, these seem to have broken down very frequently and in many cases, aides are treating patients without any supervision or training. More puzzling is the fact that the more senior staff, from the team leaders (usually senior aides) to the fully trained professionals, do not seem to participate in these groups, being largely preoccupied with other duties mainly in the administrative sphere. In other words, it would seem to me that administrative efficiency is taking precedence over patient care as far as psychotherapy is concerned.

The program policy committee, which includes the superintendent, the four unit chiefs, two members from staff development and community education, and several administrators, meets twice a week. This does not appear to be a decision-making body although it makes recommendations. The superintendent has the final decision-making power in central administration and the unit chiefs in their own particular clinical areas. I felt that the superintendent tended to make unilateral decisions, and his veto power did somewhat diminish the interest and emotional investment in making recommendations on policy. In fairness to him, it seemed that he was moving toward more shared decision making, but this subject is still controversial. He questions the validity of consensus, seeing it as time consuming and not usually practicable. At the same time, he makes every effort to get relevant inputs so that his decisions are heavily weighted by the recommendation from the people who are nearest to the problem. During my stay, it was suggested that there might be a third weekly meeting of the policy program committee to look at interpersonal difficulties. It was clear that there were many unresolved problems in this area. This was now being recognized by the establishment of a group process workshop involving the program policy committee and a few others in a three-day workshop let by Patricia Bull, a national training lab consultant, and John Tunney. I was told that this workshop was focusing on interpersonal problems at this level. Next week the team leaders and other senior staff, numbering approximately 60, will be subjected to similar learning process experience. This trend relieved some of my anxiety about the preoccupation with administrative efficiency, with the possible risk of overlooking process and social learning.

I was present at a meeting of the hospital visiting committee and was impressed by the relationship they had with the superintendent. They were interested in ASH and concerned particularly about patient welfare. Richard Steinman was outstanding, and his plans to take a sabbatical year from his post as professor of social welfare at the University of Maine to spend 15 months looking at social welfare in Scotland were announced.

I also saw the patient council in action. This group meets once a week and again, the relationship with the superintendent seemed to be open and friendly. He was a strong supporter of the role of the patient advocate. This is a full-time appointment with pay and was filled by a young man, an ex-patient who seemed to act as an ombudsman, being available to patients in their own "world" and helping them to communicate with the staff. In brief, I felt that the administration was efficient, but that the majority of senior staff was largely preoccupied with this dimension at the expense of patient care.

II. CLINICAL SERVICES (INTRAMURAL). As indicated above, the clinical services were not particularly impressive. One got the impression that the doctors operated in the traditional manner, seeing patients individually in their offices. The information learned in these treatment situations did not seem to be relayed too successfully throughout the staff, so that their knowledge of patients was limited. Nor did the psychiatrists and psychologists participate frequently in meetings where sharing of information could have been maximized. There were usually unit staff meetings once a week on most of the units, but I did not feel that these were developed to look at interpersonal problems or give the aides a significant say in planning or in social learning. On the whole, the aides seem to have become reconciled to this situation, saying that the doctors were so busy that they had no time to become involved in any interactions with patients at ward level. Many of the aides seemed to be well motivated and intelligent, but without exception, they seemed to have a feeling of frustration in relation to teaching. They also felt resentful about the way in which decisions were made centrally, and, although they might have to carry out these decisions, they had no part in the decision-making process. One example was the new record policy. This had been worked up by the program policy committee and was the third or fourth time that the record system had been changed in recent years. It was now up to the aides to fill the record forms and they felt very "left out" and resentful about carrying out something they had no investment in. Unilateral decisions from above seemed to be quite common—in fact, more so than any shared decision-making process, and I think this is a serious factor in the relatively poor morale with the aides as a body. This seems to be all the more relevant in view of the fact that most of the more active patients have been discharged, and the residual population is largely made up of institutionalized, chronic schizophrenics whose passivity would tax the best of staffs.

I participated in community meetings in each of the four units. These meetings consisted of all the patients on a particular team, of which there were three or four in each unit, interacting with the relevant staff. In some units this was a totally new experience; the only group work previously having been the aides with their five or six patients who were assigned to them in no planned way (randomly) and with no supervision. In these community meetings, the group skills were unimpressive. This is no reflection on the aides and other staff members, but merely demonstrates the lack of training opportunity they have been exposed to. In my opinion, each team should have, if possible, a daily community meeting followed by a staff review when what people said, and how they said it could be examined with the most skilled facilitator available as a teacher. Staff development has planned to have a facilitator available for each of the four units, and this may make quite a difference in the clinical skills, and the understanding of the subtlety of relationships with varying types of patients. Many of the aides said that they had never had any basic training in psychiatry and were not even clear about the various diagnostic categories. Two attempts were made in recent years to establish training teams, but these were not satisfactory and were disbanded, apparently without very much having been learned from their failure.

III. CLINICAL SERVICES (EXTRAMURAL). I was not able to visit any of the community mental health clinics (this was corrected on a later visit) and so have no first-hand knowledge in this area. However, some of the clinic personnel did come to the meetings I attended and seemed to have, themselves, many difficulties from the point of view of the organization of the clinics. I was told that each of the clinic personnel had a specific job and had little investment in the treatment program as a whole. They were not "generalists" and only had to do one particular chore, social welfare or whatever, without having the responsibility for the patient's treatment as a whole. I was also told that at least one clinic tended to select middle-class, articulate patients and had little interest in the type of chronic schizophrenic referred to them from ASH. This seemed to present a rather ridiculous contradiction—ASH trying to get all its chronic patients back into the community, and at the same time, at least in some cases, the community represented by the community mental health center showing little interest in this type of patient. Whether some of them failed to get their drugs as prescribed, and tended to drift into obscurity is not yet really known.

IV. STAFF DEVELOPMENT AND COMMUNITY EDUCATION. I never really got a clear idea of the latter organization which has, I think, six or seven people under Barbara Mayer. The three or four school teachers sounded like a good idea for educating patients who had fallen behind in their grades. It seemed that the teachers had about two patients each morning and afternoon, and even the rehabilitation workshop, which was largely woodwork, had only two patients in the morning and in the afternoon at that time, although they were able to take a total of twelve. Moreover, the link between community education and the various clinical teams seemed to be far from satisfactory. Many of the aides did not seem to be aware of the opportunities available, and even the patient advocate very honestly admitted that he was not making the best possible use of these opportunities for education in people who had fallen behind.

Staff development itself had seven full-time members. I was impressed by the opportunity for education presented by the videotape machine run by Gene and Walter. The department seems to be in a stage of transition as indeed is the whole of ASH. The plan of dividing the hospital into the four geographical units seems to be relatively new and staff development is only now beginning to organize itself around these four treatment units. This department has a long way to go, and has not yet got much skill in dealing with its own interpersonal problems. It would seem to me that this would be a first priority so that they can then go on to helping with the interpersonal problems on the teams. I found them delightful people and very willing to learn. Leadership seemed to lie with Dr. Jacobsohn and Druscilla Little, both of whom were well liked and respected. But the department's goals were not as yet too clear. I think that they see their first priority as teaching in the classroom, the effectiveness of which I have no way of assessing, not having seen any of this program. Their second priority seemed to be to become involved in the four units and to try to act as facilitators in that field. But this seemed to be a comparatively new area for most of them, and they were far from comfortable in the community meetings I attended. Even in the possible role of supervisor to the aides in their group work, there seemed to be a lack of preparedness. I have a feeling that all personnel in staff development need more exposure to group work, both in theory and practice, although this may not apply to the more senior experienced members.

The split between staff development and community education was not apparently being used as a learning situation. I do not know much about this difficulty, but it seemed necessary that it should be resolved in some way so that the 12 or 14 people involved in the two departments should be more complementary.

Conclusion

In summary, I would say that this is a remarkably promising state hospital in transition. They have an outstandingly able superintendent who is aware of the need to improve his group process skills. He tends to make unilateral decisions and as a result evokes much hostility, which to me seems unnecessary. There is not as yet much opportunity for this hostility, which permeates the whole system, to be brought into open discussion and used as a learning situation.

If ASH becomes more of an open system—and the trend is certainly there—I feel that it might become a most exciting model for change. How far staff development can help to facilitate change is an open question, but I feel that Dr. Jacobsohn is capable of this, provided he gets some strengthening of his team in staff development. How far the clinical teams will accept help from this department remains to be seen, and this, in turn, will be a measure of the willingness of the unit chiefs to participate in the evolution of an open system. The indications are that each of them, in his own way, will allow a good deal of change, but a fairly traditional attitude toward control permeates the whole system. Related to this is the relatively low level of trust that has been achieved to date. Delegation of responsibility and authority is certainly not, as yet, one of the outstanding characteristics of this hospital.

The weak link at present seems to be with the community mental health services. The official policy is to continue to move patients outward and perhaps, although it is not explicitly stated, close down all the 24-hour beds. The fact that there is no policy to absorb all the staff who might be out of work into the new community services creates considerable anxiety among the aides. I think some statement about job security at the central administrative level would do much to relieve this kind of anxiety. My own feeling is that the state hospital will not disappear in the foreseeable future at least. It may well tend to become something of a social resource, taking social casualties, including physical casualties, into its supportive embrace. The problem of the chronic patient and the future of mental hospitals is universal in the United States, and if it is going to be worked out anywhere, I think ASH will be in a leading position as an experimenter and creator of a new model.

Turning now to the more general problem of "chronic" mental patients, it is hard to reconcile health with the picture presented by the "institutionalized" chronic schizophrenic patient who now represents the majority of patients left in our state hospitals. The more "progressive" hospitals have "rehabilitated" many, or in some instances, most of their previous patients to life in the general population. This move may have been inspired by political and economic motives as much as for humanitarian reasons, for many ex-mental hospital patients now languish in circumstances little, if any, better than those they experienced in the "back wards" of a state hospital.[1]

It seems to me that the move to liquidate the state hospitals in favor of a "community" life for the mentally handicapped misses the point. We are in danger of substituting the stigma of "institutionalization" for the equally dangerous situation of "rootlessness." Many ex-mental hospital patients are now living a marginal existence, not unlike the fate of first generation emigrants at the turn of the century. Unable to relate to the general community in the passive-dependent role relationship to staff that characterizes "institutionalization," they often seek readmittance to the familiar supportive environment of the state hospital or accept a compromise in the form of a boarding or nursing home run as a private enterprise for profit. An unknown number "disappear" from the records, so their fate is largely a matter of conjecture. Some give up and kill themselves; some come to the attention of the police, and whether they end up in prison or are "recycled" through a state hospital it may merely be a matter of chance. Some turn to drink or drugs to escape from a life of isolation, while some "enjoy" varying degrees of care and support

[1]Maxwell Jones, "Community Care for Chronic Mental Patients. The Need for a Reassessment," *Hospital & Community Psychiatry* 26 (1975): 94–98.

from community mental health centers or other welfare agencies.

For this residue of institutionalized patients, we need to ask ourselves, as did Fairweather, in what circumstances and in what social organization will their limited capacities have most chance for fulfillment and even growth?[2] The value of a supportive and understanding peer group in this context has been stressed throughout this book, as has the value of resource people (facilitators) who may have a professional training that enables them to help the consumers to help themselves.

It seems to me that the discredited state hospital has never had a chance to realize its potential as a system for change in the direction of patient health. The first and perhaps the most serious mistake was to establish hospitals for the treatment of mental patients. The preoccupation with pathology lead to the somewhat artificial identification of symptoms and the creation of disease entities. The jibe that the role of the patient is to be "sick" had a certain validity and equated with that preconception, admission to hospital often tended to reinforce "illness" patterns that were communicated and in a sense "taught" to patients and relatives by staff members.[3]

Along with this "medical" orientation, a whole host of apparent irrelevancies can be identified. Why is a medical director someone who in many state hospitals wields immense power and in some cases has learned his administrative skills on the job and occasionally almost overnight (when transferred from the clinical services)? Why are M.D.s the most highly paid and usually the most powerful group of professionals? Why are all the characteristics of a closed system commonplace? Closed systems are charac-

[2]G. W. Fairweather, *Methods of Experimental Social Innovation* (New York: John Wiley & Sons, 1967).

[3]Paul Polak and Maxwell Jones, "The Psychiatric Non-Hospital: A Model for Change," *Community Mental Health Journal* 9 (1973): 123–32.

terized by (a) little evidence of two-way communication throughout the system, especially from the consumer—patients and their relatives—to the people at the top where much of the responsibility and power is found, (b) little opportunity for patients and lower echelons of staff to participate in decision making that effects them directly, (c) little opportunity to explore problems at ward level with a view to social learning and growth. In brief, the role of the patient is largely equated with passive dependency, with little expectation or opportunity for self-help or creative interaction with their peers and junior staff. Not only is "treatment" controlled by the professional staff who decide which of numerous competing methodologies is "best" for the patient, but even his daytime activities are planned for him. Admittedly in Europe some relatively "healthy" individuals in hospital choose to go on vacation tours in which virtually everything is planned for them by the staff, but at least the initial choice is theirs, and if they learn little or nothing about the people and the country of their choice, they have only themselves to blame!

I had the experience of trying to establish an open system in a mental hospital in Scotland. As physician superintendent, I had the power and authority to sanction change, and in seven years in this post, acting as facilitator, I helped the authority and responsibility to be delegated throughout the system including both patients and staff.

Fort Logan Mental Health Center, in Denver, Colorado started 14 years ago and the social organization from the start was relatively "open." As a result, the contact with the patients' community has always been a significant factor in the systems approach, and this has helped to keep the number of 24-hour patients to a minimum—less than 200 inpatients, although Fort Logan serves an area of approximately one million people. Despite the fact that Fort Logan clearly represents a breakthrough in relation to the function of state hospitals, it has had no imitators to date.

This resistance to change in state hospitals and psychiatric facilities generally—medical school psychiatry departments, Veteran's Administration Hospitals, private psychiatric hospitals, nursing and boarding homes, etc.—is in line with the resistance to change manifested by virtually all social organizations. In other words, the human race is conditioned to conformity and unquestioning acceptance of existing practices from the beginning of life, and is ill-equipped to become part of a change system. The dynamics of change has been the major thesis of Part I of this book. Can these principles already found in part at two psychiatric hospitals—Fort Logan in Denver and Dingleton in Scotland—be applied to psychiatric facilities in general, with a view to affording more opportunities of self-fulfillment and growth to mental health casualties?

The present position in relation to state hospitals is absurd and reflects the relative demoralization of the whole of psychiatry. These institutions are regarded by most people as an evil necessity, if only to protect society from its own negative image. Fisher, et al., give a dramatic account of the problems facing state hospitals and the almost impossible task of achieving a growth process toward health for the majority of long-term inmates.[4]

There is no easy short-term answer to the dilemma of the state hospital. To abolish it as an anachronism, as is the trend in some states, is to expose our lack of valid information and capacity to plan a more effective system of care and change in the direction of health. Nor are the more imaginative plans to develop a community care system, e.g., community mental health centers, particularly satisfactory, especially in relation to the social casualties often categorized as "chronic patients."

Community care plans evolved almost overnight, in part as a reaction to the discrepancy between the psychiatric treatment facilities available to the rich and the poor in

[4]W. Fisher, J. Mehr, and P. Truckenbrod, *Power, Greed and Stupidity in the Mental Health Racket* (Philadelphia: Westminster Press, 1973).

the United States. The late President John F. Kennedy in a message to Congress in 1963 stated, "I propose a national mental health program to assist in the inauguration of a wholly new emphasis and approach to care for the mentally ill. Governments at every level, federal, state, and local, private foundations, and individual citizens must all face up to their responsibilities in this area."[5] The high hopes for this new "community" orientation for psychiatry have not been fully realized. Among the many reasons for this was the basic assumption that part responsibility for mental health could be "wished" on an unsuspecting public who had had no opportunity to participate in the planning stages.

The lack of complementarity between the plans to abolish state hospitals and the rise of community mental health centers is stressed by Braceland.

> Admittedly a number of state hospitals are wretched places. Legislatures have starved them for years and many were even unable to make a decent habitat for the sick human beings sent to them. But this was not psychiatry's fault—it was the fault of citizens who allowed it to happen. When things did happen, however, psychiatrists were made the scapegoats for not doing what they had been asking for money to do, year after year with no results.
>
> No reasonable person can fail to see the value of the community health center concept. Any project that will keep patients out of state hospitals is most welcome, provided it cares for and tries to rehabilitate the patient while he lives in other decent, protected surroundings.[6]

The examples of a systems approach in a medical school psychiatric unit and a state hospital demonstrate the

[5]John F. Kennedy, "Message from the President of the United States Relative to Mental Illness and Mental Retardation," 88th Congress, 1st Session, House of Representatives, 5 February, 1963, Document No. 58.

[6]Francis J. Braceland, Introductory Remarks to "Psychiatry under Siege," *Psychiatric Annals* 3, 11 November, 1973.

role of the facilitator in a short (two-week) exposure to a social system. Ideally an outside consultant remains with a system until such time as his purpose, as perceived by both the system and the facilitator, has been realized, or the process reaches the point where the system feels competent to reach these goals without further help from him.

A Community Mental Health Center

The following example traces the growth of a relatively closed system to an open system in a community mental health center in Denver. The time span covers the period March 1972 to the end of 1973. The original contract was for the facilitator (myself) to be present for six to eight weekly staff meetings, but in June 1972 the staff meeting reached consensus that the facilitator was still necessary and he was asked to continue for the time being. In January 1973 the team and the outside facilitator agreed that alternate leaders (facilitators) had emerged in the team, so that they felt competent to operate as an open system without an outside facilitator. An unusual aspect of this situation was the fact that I was paid by Fort Logan Mental Health Center, but allowed to operate as a facilitator to other developing mental health clinics in Denver as an extension of staff development at Fort Logan, which was the state hospital for the Denver area. This circumstance contributed to the team's request that the facilitator continue to attend the staff meetings in the role of an "honorary member." My experience of developing systems in mental health was seen as relevant to their plans for a much extended community outreach program, including C&E (consultation and education). This honorary member role in the outreach commitee, included planning a systems approach to local schools, helping in seminars on systems theory to businessmen, church groups, etc. This transition is important as it afforded the facilitator an opportunity to operate both as an outside consultant and to some extent as a facilitator from within the system.

Example of Facilitator Role in a Mental Health Center

On March 23, 1972, a colleague, Margaret Weeks, and I, from the staff development department at Fort Logan, went as outside consultants to Bethesda Community Mental Health Center (the "Center" for short) in Denver, serving a population of approximately 100,000 people. Several of the staff of approximately 25 professionals had at some time previously worked at Fort Logan and were well known to us.

This particular center was started in August 1969 and had a hospital inpatient service of 70 beds run by some 17 psychiatrists who were in private practice. The hospital service dated from 1949 and was primarily designed to treat psychotic patients.

The invitation to attend a one-day workshop as consultants came from the program director (team leader) John DeHaan, but was approved by the head of the Bethesda organization, Bill Scholten, a psychiatrist, and the members of the community mental health center team.

The center had 15 beds for those patients who needed hospital care. These patients were under the care of one of the center's psychiatrists, but they were admitted to available beds scattered throughout the hospital service.

The Center staff comprised two M.D.s, twelve M.S.W.s, two psychologists, three R.N.s, and six paraprofessionals.

At the time of the workshop there had been some attempt at delegation of responsibility and authority. During the previous six months, there had been a movement from central management to indirect management by regularly scheduled meetings with the coordinators and the central authority. These coordinators were the heads of the inpatient service, outpatients, aftercare, and day care. My notes of this one-day workshop were as follows:

> Margaret and I were identified as facilitators for the meeting. Meeting started at 9:20 A.M.—long silence. A junior staff member suggested that there were problems in relation to the authority structure. This brought in John DeHaan, program director, and Bill Scholten, M.D., medical director of Bethesda. It soon became evident that no one was clear as to what the social organization at Bethesda Community Mental Health Clinic really was or its exact relationship with the authority structure. We learned that the hierarchy is (1) Bethesda Hospital Association; (2) B. H. Citizens Advisory Board; (3) Bill (medical director); (4) John (program director); (5) the four coordinators of inpatients, outpatients, aftercare, and day care departments; (6) clinical personnel.
>
> Communication and decision making were discussed. It was felt that both were tending to improve and more people were involved. The issue of one of the three inpatient wards being used exclusively for Center patients was discussed. The Center staff said they heard via the ward nurses that the suggestion was turned down and the Center was not even involved in the discussions. John (program director) admitted that this was an example of bad decision making. He would like to make decisions through the weekly meetings of coordinators. There is a weekly meeting of the whole mental health center staff, but this is not a decision-making body and is not attended by Bill, the medical director of both the Center and the hospital. The meeting is primarily for inservice training.
>
> Bruce, one of the paraprofessional staff, then "risked" communicating his problem regarding a pay raise and taking over Betsy's more responsible job when she leaves. He was angry with John, and to a lesser extent, with the two coordinators to whom he was referred by John. John admitted he needed time to collect his answers, but was in error in not calling a meeting with himself and the two coordinators (not Bruce). I suggested that John was more comfortable with his peers than in an open confrontation with Bruce. John got "strokes" for his honesty; also the two coordinators for ex-

pressing their feelings. We began to see interaction which had the makings of a learning situation.

Margaret (facilitator) summarized our progress and the increasing "openness" of the meeting. This helped two female nurses to talk about their feelings and need for support. Betsy began talking about her plans to leave which had deeply affected the nurses.

After lunch people wanted to continue to discuss Betsy's reasons for leaving. At first she had been glad to escape from the "sharing of feelings" expected at Fort Logan before she joined the Center staff, but now she had second thoughts. She felt she was not learning and growing at Bethesda and felt "unfulfilled." She felt her work was not appreciated and she was getting no recognition or appreciation from the senior staff.

One of the psychiatrists had been absent most of the A.M., and in view of the general criticism of the team leadership, I tried to raise his role relationship with John and the plight of the three M.D.s—Glen, Charles, and Bill. I got jumped on for introducing a new topic and the climate was tense. Margaret came to my rescue and talked about the role of a consultant and how continuity (process) might have to be halted temporarily to crystallize some point for retention (learning). For a time there seemed to be a danger of the "sensitivity training" element taking over and certainly there appeared to be a reluctance to discuss M.D.s. Bill, the medical director of Bethesda, appealed for help regarding M.D.s and this appeared to "sanction" discussion of their role. Charles got strokes by appealing for feedback regarding his performance and effectiveness and responding well to painful communication. This brought Glen in, in a very positive way. He felt lack of support and understanding regarding his very difficult and relatively isolated role as psychiatrist to the Center's inpatient service. The Center's interest was mainly directed away from the inpatients to the outside community. A coordinator gave a good example of painful communication in discussing Charles' role. He operated like most clinical psychiatrists, not sharing information with the R.N.'s, etc., and not seeking information from them.

Margaret summarized the important issues raised as follows:

1. The all day workshops (think days) to continue and be held approximately every two months.
2. The rehashes following patient/staff or staff/staff meeting to be held regularly to enhance skills in social learning.
3. The Senior staff Coordinators' meeting to be held weekly to improve communications, planning and decision making.
4. Feedback from the above coordinators meeting to a weekly full team meeting to enhance this process of social learning to all team members.
5. The consensus was that the weekly team meeting (1½ hours) had been a wasted opportunity for learning up to now.
6. Bill said he'd attend the weekly team meeting.

Margaret and I were asked if we could continue in the roles of facilitators.

The meeting ended in a very positive mood.

I felt it was very positive meeting because:

1. It was the first ever meeting of the whole staff specifically to examine and discuss the social organization.
2. The meeting got down to work immediately by looking at authority structure.
3. Joe, one of the coordinators, offered himself early as "sacrificial lamb" or "risk-taker", and so initiated a process of social learning.
4. John responded well to criticism of the authority structure and so "sanctioned" further discussion of his (and Bill's) role.
5. Trust in the group's integrity became part of the process of growth.
6. Bruce, a paraprofessional staff member, "risked" discussing his dissatisfaction with John, and helped to bridge the gap between senior and junior staff.
7. Two R.N.'s wept and discussed their feelings of lack of support—they got positive strokes from the group.
8. At the coffee break, there apparently was much positive interaction between all levels of staff.
9. The Group was confident enough to criticize my inputs, which incidentally served to show that risk-taking can be helpful and lead to positive interaction and learning.

10. Betsy's discussion of leaving the Center helped to focus on the staff's unfulfilled emotional needs and this became everyone's responsibility.
11. A "feelings meeting" climate was seen as unproductive unless it focused on concrete (clinical) issues so that everyone was clear as to the subject matter, and the discussion was not delving into "personal" issues too much.
12. Bill and John, the two senior staff members, changed their image as seen by the staff as a whole. This was partly due to a structure (think day) which allowed them plenty of time to communicate and become human beings.
13. The same process applied to M.D.'s.
14. The focus of the meeting (communication, social learning and decision-making) and their potential for social learning became "real" and not just academic.
15. The advantage of two facilitators was demonstrated to me. Margaret's support, understanding, and skill freed me to make "risk-taking" inputs to facilitate the change process in a limited (one day) workshop.
16. John saw us as impartial, in our roles as facilitators.
17. Margaret and I were asked to continue to act as facilitators.

Following a three-week delay I joined the staff meeting at Bethesda as a facilitator. My notes dated April 13, 1972 ran as follows:

> Staff development at Fort Logan had decided that I take up Bethesda's request for a consultant for six to eight weekly staff meetings as a facilitator and that other people, especially Margaret, could not be spared. The head of the alcohol program started the meeting by commenting on the silence and disease. The meeting focused on Charles, a psychiatrist who had felt hurt that a decision to have an outside facilitator for the staff meetings had been taken in his absence. Apparently he is seen as the chairman of the staff meetings on Thursdays, which had no clearly defined function other than inservice training. Charles agreed that the process started at the one-day workshop should be continued in the weekly staff meetings.

> We then spent about 30 minutes in sweetness and light and when I commented on what looked like "avoiding" tactics, one of the coordinators began to talk about her feelings of frustration. Apparently she and John agreed to her developing an aftercare program, but she was given only five hours per week to do this. Since that time, two other staff members had been given half time to develop this project. The coordinator, weeping, admitted that she felt envious of their freedom to do the very thing she would have liked to have done herself. She likened her condition to having adopted a child that other people were looking after. John felt he had been mistaken in making this decision with the coordinator and not sharing the planning of the aftercare program with the whole staff. He added that he felt that minor decisions should be made by him as team leader to spare staff time. He seems determined to have decision making by consensus when possible and practicable, and this seemed to fit in with the wish for the meeting to be partly training in social learning and O.D. I suggested that we don't just discuss the coordinator's feelings, but we try to operate as a decision-making body too. These meetings must be more than just talking. The climate seemed very positive and various people stressed the good effect on morale which they attributed in part to the workshop on March 23.

In retrospect, it seems to me that I was operating more as an interventionist than a facilitator, at both the initial workshop and my first staff meeting. The staff seemed to be ready to examine their social organization with a view to evolving a more open system of communication and decision making. The program director or team leader, John DeHaan, a social worker by training, was interested in social systems and had circulated a document a few weeks before the initial workshop under his name giving his views on management. This document affords a unique glimpse at the program director's perception of his role at that time and his perception of the social organization of the Center.

Basically, he supported the model of participant management but with the power and control firmly at the top.

Delegation was described as the act of placing decision-making responsibility at the level closest to where the action takes place. The appropriate response of the program director to a decision he disagreed with was to convince the subordinates to change their decision. If unable to do this, he should (a) accept and live with the decision, (b) change the decision maker. There was no attention given to learning through social interaction or to process, although such possibilities may have been implied.

The document goes on to say that the administration has a number of alternatives from which to choose when making decisions.

1. *Management by consensus* is the preferred method of decision making when:

   a. The decision has significant influence on those within the boundary.
   b. The decision has only intramural implications.
   c. The decision needs a broad base of support.

2. *Management by directive* is the preferred method of decision making when:

   a. Speed is essential.
   b. Highly technical issues are involved.
   c. Insignificant material is considered.
   d. Involvement is not practical.
   e. Procedures have not been formalized or are not being followed.
   f. Executive directives are needed.
   g. Consensus is not feasible.

This document is significant in indicating the team leader's concept of his authority role and the extent to which decision making could be shared. It was circulated to team members a few weeks before our first workshop. It provoked no discussion, and when at one of the early weekly staff meetings I questioned their apparent disinterest in its contents, the staff showed no interest in discussing their reactions to John's theories on management. At the same time, the first workshop on March 23, 1972 began by an active discussion of John's behavior as team leader and by implication of his ineptness in not arriving at a shared decision with the relevant people and not developing a learning situation. But the process in the initial stages of the workshop demonstrated his willingness to learn by experience and to willingly admit his mistakes without becoming defensive.

This is an early example of social learning at Bethesda. John's written account of his concept of management in relation to his role as leader, and his relationship to the team had no perceptible effect on team members. A discussion involving everyone in an interactional situation at the workshop had a significant effect on John's image of himself and as he was seen by the team.

Some of the changes toward an open system are described as they occurred chronologically.

JUNE 8, 1972—CONFRONTATION AND DECISION MAKING. At the staff meeting, John, program director, gave feedback from the previous coordinator's meeting of the previous day and added that Glen was now to become the senior psychiatrist, i.e., to have more authority than his colleague Charles. This unilateral decision was immediately challenged and neither John nor Glen were able to allay the anxiety and anger of their peers at being bypassed in the decision-making process. Charles was obviously discomforted, not so much by the decision since he was thinking of leaving anyway, but by a process that seemed to devalue him. John felt that the facts were being misrepresented, but failed to convince the team. The tension remained high and the meeting time was almost over. As it seemed clear that the issue involved shared decision making, the facilitator suggested an emergency meeting as soon as possible. This was agreed to and scheduled for the following Tuesday. The facilitator was asked to attend and agreed to do so.

SEPTEMBER 7, 1972—LEVELING THE AUTHORITY STRUCTURE. Bill Scholten, as the medical director of Bethesda, both the hospital and the Center, had the most powerful position in the clinical team. At the initial workshop on March 23, 1972, he had expressed his willingness to attend the weekly Center staff meetings but had not done so until August 10. This appearance was partly as a result of mounting pressure from the team for his presence and his own need for support in his lonely position at the top of the hierarchy. His presence inevitably changed the group atmosphere as he was still largely unknown to his staff and the level of trust had not yet been clarified. Mary Ann (a nurse) questioned the effect that Bill and John (the two senior staff members) had on the staff meetings—without their presence the climate was much more relaxed. Bill followed up by saying he realized that to some extent at least, he had a negative image and described a scene that took place several months previously when he had lost his temper with a paraprofessional. Mary Ann had been present at this fracas and had been terrified. The facilitator pointed out that the social organization at that time provided no opportunity to turn this crisis into a learning situation. The facilitator helped Bill to talk about his difficulty in wearing two hats. In the hospital system he played the largely traditional authoritarian role that was expected of him by the hierarchy. In the community mental health center, with its growth toward the sharing of responsibility and authority, quite a different role was expected.

The climate in the staff meeting was now much less tense and this was probably a factor in helping Bill to share some of his loneliness and feeling of vulnerability with the group. This process of sharing seemed to please most people, and his eagerness for support, understanding, and help led to some staff saying how much more positive his image now was for them.

NOVEMBER 9, 1972—AN EFFECTIVE WORKSHOP Much preparatory work had been done by the coordinators for this 9:00 A.M. to 2:00 P.M. workshop: (a) Summary of Goals of Bethesda as perceived by the staff; (b) Summary of staff hours for September, 1972, i.e., the percentage of staff time on all activities under the general headings of direct service (51.1 per cent), indirect service (41.5 percent), and fringe costs (holidays, etc.) 7.4 per cent; (c) Summary of findings of a door-to-door survey to explore community needs in the Bethesda area.

(a) The goals of Bethesda stressed community prevention programs including psychosocial indices to help in planning and evaluation, e.g., suicide rates, school dropout rates, number and geographical distribution of families on welfare, rates of alcohol and drug abuse, divorce rates, etc. Among the most frequently raised issues were the need for more involvement in planning.

(b) An analysis of how staff spent their time expressed as a percentage of the total time available was computed.

The Center had available 15 hospital beds at Bethesda which were never fully utilized. One-third of the total monies available were spent on this hospital service. But in order to indicate where the staff priorities lay, time was seen as a better indicator than money. In direct service (51.5 per cent) most time went to adult and adolescent outpatient care, day treatment, and inpatient care, in that order. Indirect service (41.5 per cent) showed in-service training, administration, and community services in that order, although the latter accounted for only 4.1 per cent of the total staff time available. The remaining 7.4 per cent was accounted for by public holidays and vacation time.

(c) The uncompleted results of a community survey

showed some interesting trends as to how the local population expressed their needs. These included information about what mental health resources are available, a crisis center for kids, halfway house for runaways, day care for family members of working mothers, more creative outlets for nonworking mothers, etc. There was only one general practitioner in the area and medical problems such as medicaid care, birth control information, nursing care for the elderly were stressed. Neighborhood complaints included deteriorating residences and fear of high rise apartments taking over, poor recreational facilities, vandalism, and danger in the streets at night.

The three reports were circulated before the workshop. At the coordinator's weekly meeting held one day before, the expectation was that the workshop would afford a mutual sharing of ideas and the pulling together of the guidelines could be left to the coordinators. This suggested that the major planning and decision-making functions at the Center were still seen as being mainly a senior staff concern.

I was accompanied by Margaret Weeks from Fort Logan who had acted as a co-facilitator at our initial all-day workshop on March 23, 1972.

The meeting started with a discussion of valid data.

After further information exchange, the chairman asked if the theme was direct service vs. a community mental health program. But the group needed time for information sharing. Glen, a psychiatrist, felt that one-third of total budget going to inpatient services was excessive, especially when only 4.1 percent of staff time was available for community services. He felt a more efficient link with the hospital system could be developed (not necessarily a separate inpatient unit for the Center). The group now began to discuss what they meant by community treatment and mentioned family care, halfway houses, crisis intervention, and hospital alternatives.

A coffee break seemed timely!! People still seemed to be avoiding the crucial issue—do they want to develop community services?

After the coffee break, the coordinator for aftercare seemed to be the logical person to start the discussion on the need to further develop a community program. She talked about a multipurpose clinic—crisis intervention—using existing facilities. Bill, the medical director, commented on developing indirect services, using nontreatment personnel. The aftercare coordinator was not sure of the potential resources in the community but felt optimistic. The team resisted facing the extent of their internal commitment to community psychiatry. Three experienced staff members elaborated on the difficulties which included isolation, frustration, and lack of professional support. An R.N. said, "I don't know how to change a community; I'm scared." I (as facilitator) spoke about the crisis unit at Fort Logan and the community program at Dingleton Hospital in Scotland which was structured to enhance learning with frequent multidisciplinary seminars. A staff member came back to internal commitment. Another offered an educational program that aimed at the prevention of alcoholism. The aftercare coordinator wanted to know who coordinated the programs, e.g., kids, alcohol, etc. Some of the group seemed to feel she was seeking power, but John pointed out that she constantly sounds out the group to inquire if she's going in the right direction. Margaret (facilitator) pointed out that she had not yet had an answer —what priority does the group give to community services? Internal commitment to community psychiatry includes people in the Center who will have to pick up other's cases.

Noon: I pointed out resistance to change, e.g., if they decided to increase community commitments, then every individual role might be affected. We seemed to be stuck. Evolution may be best route—the aftercare coordinator has to feed valid information from the community and people will become involved, in their own way, in their own time. Bill wanted to look at structure, e.g., a coordinator of the whole community program. Should this be the aftercare coordinator or who? Margaret felt that looking for a coordinator was to avoid conflict still in a group. (This was in part a criticism of my evolutionary action position and an "action-oriented interventionist role" vs. Margaret's "process role." I felt justified in playing this role, as the second facilitator was avoiding intervention or involvement, being content to comment on process.)

Lunch: On resuming we seemed to achieve consensus on getting a structure that would allow the community system to grow. The aftercare coordinator wondered if the conflict was being blown up because we were really committed to a community program but didn't know how to get it done. John began to focus on conflict. Bill spoke of the value of the community coordinator concept in resolving conflict. But the group seemed to want to examine where everyone stood on priorities—staff development, program evaluation, C&E (consultation and education). I questioned if we were now talking about C&E rather than community psychiatry (as had been discussed in the morning). Could this indicate a resistance to the head of aftercare as coordinator of the community program? We could go this route (conflict) or, in the hour left for discussion, focus on structure for, say C&E, which could become a model for change. (I was probably trying to influence the group toward action planning). The group preferred to continue getting inputs regarding individual priorities. This was a very time-consuming subject, and the chairman tested the group's readiness to move on. She suggested that we set up a structure and test where individuals wanted to commit themselves. Margaret interrupted and said only one-third had spoken. This was probably an overstatement and may have indicated Margaret's feeling that conflict resolution still was necessary before action planning (I was always in a hurry). So feedback continued and staff development was given as first priority by several people. The chairman saw staff development as a logical start for community work. By 1:35 P.M. we finished going round getting priorities.

With a few minutes left, John tried an action approach. If Brian would take over the halfway house project, this would free the aftercare coordinator as community coordinator. Someone questioned why her. John suggested the formation of an interested group (ad hoc steering committee for three months to feed back to the larger group) to evolve a program. He was prepared to act as co-chairman with the aftercare coordinator, learning by doing, but also by sharing and planning. I (with my admitted bias) saw this as excellent timing on John's part and the fact that the group seemed to be in agreement with his plan suggested that there had been sufficient problem solving to allow the group to move on to action planning.

This workshop showed how the authority structure (the coordinators) made every effort to give valid information to the total staff and test their perception as to priorities, and in particular, to explore their willingness to spend more time in extending their program in the direction of community involvement. The resistance to this greater commitment, which would inevitably affect every staff member, seemed to take the form of prolonged information sharing and examination of conflict. Disagreement between the two facilitators (myself and Margaret) became evident when I reinforced the action planners, while Margaret continued to focus on process, feeling that the group was not yet ready for action. The effect was a lessening rather than a heightening of tension in the group, and this readiness to "move" was exemplified by John in his capacity of program director, who in the closing minutes, suggested an ad hoc group with shared leadership to evolve a community program and report back to the staff meeting.

In fact, this ad hoc committee is still in existence and welcomes any staff member who is interested in community planning and action. John's restrained but effective style of leadership was evident at this workshop and his increasing tendency to share decision making and avoid unilateral action was seen. His timing in the final minutes was very effective. Finally, the complementarity made possible by using two facilitators was interesting. I felt free to play a more active "risk taking" role, than had I been on my own.

A CHANGE IN EMPHASIS FROM ILLNESS TO HEALTH—FEBRUARY 8, 1973.

Another all-day workshop began, by three days of workshops by the coordinators who had arrived at a list of program priorities. This list gave a month-by-month record of proposals covering 12 months. As an example, the priorities proposed for March 1973 included a functioning halfway house in the community, an investigation of the possibilities for free radio and T.V. time for mental health education, a meeting with community gatekeepers (ministers, lawyers, etc.), the assignment of one person three hours per week to coordinate staff development programs, an investigation of intake systems (including crisis intervention), etc. At the time of writing a year later, these program priorities, which were modified only slightly by the staff at the workshop, have been materially realized.

At the workshop, I asked where the financial resources for the new programs were coming from, and was told that by cutting down their inpatient beds from 15 to 10, a maximum of $80,000 would be provided.

The discussion, which was largely task centered, meant that the facilitator was largely an observer, but I was able to observe as the community outreach program became more of a reality, and there was a growing trend to change the focus (and the terminology) from a preoccupation with pathology, illness, and treatment to a greater concern with health, prevention, and learning as a social process.

JULY 12, 1973—WORKSHOP 9 A.M. to 2 P.M. There had been a regression of the authority structure under stress resulting in action without interaction involving the whole staff. Conflicting priorities for the workshop discussion were a drug grant, and seven staff members who were leaving in the near future.

The anxiety level was high. Everyone knew via a written note that John and the head of the alcohol program had submitted a tentative proposal for a drug grant. They said that there had been no time to process this plan through the previous week's staff meeting as they had learned on very short notice that some grant money had become available. The possibility of submitting such an application had been discussed for months, but no decision had been reached. The issue caused much anxiety since, if successful, the new drug grant might well double the number of staff and even jeopardize the job security of members of the existing staff.

The chairman wanted to discuss this issue at the start of the meeting, but there were many other agenda items and the staff preferred to express their anxiety about so many people leaving. The departure of Mary Ellen, head of the outpatient department, in particular was seen as an irreparable loss.

Acting as a facilitator, I pointed out the need for a leader, as the staff appeared to be demoralized. John said he could not respond as he had such a close relationship with Mary Ellen and did not know how he could manage without her.

The chairman said that she was unable to read the group, but felt that people wanted to continue the process of mourning.

Some attention was now directed toward the coordinator's meetings, which took place weekly the day before the staff meeting. Their minutes were supposed to be discussed, but this often failed to materialize. I asked if on major issues, like the drug grant, decision making involved consensus from the whole staff, or if decisions were made at the coordinator's meetings. A staff member felt it was still unclear where decisions were made. John showed both frustration and anger. The tentative grant proposal had meant a few days of intense hard work, and the product had been shared with the staff in a written statement. (Incidentally it was a most imaginative document, stressing preventive measures to lessen the incidence of drug addiction.) All that he and his collaborator were getting was negative criticism, and at the same time, the staff seemed to avoid sharing responsibility. Someone mentioned in relation to Mary Ellen's leaving that John felt it would be seen as inappropriate by his peers if, in his relatively junior capacity, he competed with the much more senior head of the alcohol program for the vacancy.

I suggested that there was a crisis of leadership. John and his collaborator were being devalued, and alternate leaders were not emerging, so that the balance and security found in multiple leadership was lacking for the moment. This was linked to the general feeling of uncertainty regarding the future with so many staff leaving. It seemed that nothing was being learned in relation to the grant issue, i.e., social learning requires psychodynamic skills and not just discussion and information sharing.

John was still annoyed that the staff had not read the memos he sent them. I pointed out that reading usually affects the individual differently than discussion and interaction. Each individual tends to interpret written material in his own way (or may not read it at all), while interaction must modify everyone's position, including the initiators. He suggested that an emergency meeting of available staff might have avoided much of the distortion of facts and the anger. In the discussion it was felt that the tentative drug grant proposal might have been seriously considered had interaction with the whole staff occurred. As it was, the staff felt that no action should be taken at present, and that an application should be made at some later date if everyone on the staff was agreed on the decision. Unless consensus could be reached, the plan would have a poor chance of success.

SEPTEMBER 5, 1973—COORDINATOR'S WORKSHOP. THE CONCEPT OF "CONTAINMENT" IN RELATION TO A POWERFUL NEW M.D. LEADER WAS THE TOPIC. Rick Leet had been appointed as clinical director two months before, to fill Glen Shipley's vacancy. Glen had been quite an unobtrusive psychiatrist who had never challenged John's leadership or that of the other coordinators.

I was invited to act as facilitator at a three-hour workshop of the six coordinators.

A coordinator asked how much of Bill's power had been delegated to Rick. Bill was the medical director of Bethesda Hospital as well as the mental health center. Also, he asked how much of John's power, as program director of the Center, had been taken over by the new M.D. John, being a social worker by training, might be seen as less qualified professionally than an M.D.

Rick said he'd been told that he was one of a triumvirate, Bill, John and himself, but that details of the authority structure had not been worked out.

It was noted that Rick had prepared a new plan for more members on the coordinator's committee and had written this on the blackboard before the meeting. John had collaborated in the planning stage, but it was Rick who now seemed to be taking a leadership role and explaining the plan to the group.

A coordinator said she was not angry with Rick but couldn't figure out what was happening to John—was he hurting and not showing it?

John described the early authority structure of the Center with coordinators, including himself, making the decisions and psychiatrists only attending on request. He had tried to get Glen to attend as clinical director but Glen had tended to avoid responsibility.

Bill and John were helped to see that their familiar presence and trusted leadership were needed to reassure the staff that a psychiatrist (Rick) was not "taking over" leadership. Bill spoke about John's value as an organization man and equated this with clinical skills which in his opinion were no more important.

It was felt that Rick needed time to familiarize himself with the system and that his role should reflect his own needs and skills, but at the same time, be complementary to the needs of the Center as a whole. If Rick tended to seek more power than the staff liked, it was their responsibility to contain him, i.e., confront him with their anxiety and work through the issue.

This led to a discussion of multiple (multidisciplinary) leadership and the need for anyone to achieve leadership status in the area of his competence, no matter what his status (pay) position in the hierarchy.

It was felt that the power and responsibility was largely distributed throughout the system, but that when matters arose that related to conflict with the outside world, the formal authority structure was inevitably evoked.

John suggested that all the departmental meetings, outpatients, day care, etc., should be scheduled for Monday morning so that there was plenty of time to share minutes, etc., with the whole staff before the Thursday staff meeting.

Examples of all-day workshops have been recorded at roughly three-month intervals in an attempt to capture some of the process of change covering a period of eighteen months. They heightened the effectiveness of the weekly meetings attended by all the center staff.

The role of the interventionist was established at the start, and he was asked to help to open up communications, implement shared decision making, identify problems, and help in their resolution by a process of social learning. He felt that these objectives had been largely attained after nine months, but he agreed to the team's request to stay on. During the second period of nine months, he felt himself to be largely incorporated within the system and so acted more in the role of an alternate leader when active leadership seemed to be lacking. This is seen as compatible with the role of a facilitator working from *within* the system. The last two meetings (February and September, 1973) were periods of unusual stress and he attempted to re-establish the equilibrium of power which was consciously formulated by the team as multiple leadership and shared responsibility throughout the system.

Chapter 8

GENERAL CONSIDERATIONS

It is evident that psychiatry is in trouble and the past decade has seen a lessening of its credibility in the eyes of the general public. The high hopes of a successful breakthrough by psychoanalytic methods of treatment have dimmed, and the more recent community mental health orientation has its limitations. In line with this partial disenchantment with psychiatry, the Nixon administration planned drastic cuts in federal spending on the mental health programs. There is no short-term solution for these problems, although they may be helped by the trend to increasing community involvement in the form of community mental health clinics, family therapy, crisis intervention units, and so on. But something much more drastic would seem to be called for.

This book has emphasized the need for the development of open systems and the proper place to start, in my opinion, is in the schools. The implications of such a plan are staggering, and to many people will seem quite unrealistic. The immediate reaction of some thoughtful people might be that something is being imposed from without and a democratic orientation can be as dangerous for society as any other approach. The realization of an open systems approach would mean a social organization that aimed at the sharing of valid information, interaction with a teacher or other resource person acting as facilitator, and the identification and resolution of individual or group problems. This would imply a group process, and not the imposition of ideas through one-way communication in a closed system.

But we live in an age when power is in the hands of a small minority and the sharing of information is often limited to a few and kept a closely guarded secret. Witness the Watergate issues in the present presidential administration. If the model at the top levels of administration and industry represent relatively closed systems, what hope is there for the advocates of open systems? But the United States is a country of extraordinary contrasts, and as Revel has pointed out, may well be leading the world in the direction of change through a radically new approach to moral values.[1] He cites the black revolt, the feminist movement, the rejection by the young of technology and wealth as dominant social goals, more permissive methods in education, a feeling of guilt in relation to the underpriveleged, a desire for equality, opposition to the abuse of authority at home and abroad, and a growing awareness of the futility of war.

If learning as a social process had the same priority in schools as the acquisition of knowledge, then we would see the dawn of a new era. But first the whole educational and political system, not to mention the general public, would have to sanction (and understand) such a change in emphasis. To anticipate such a transition in the present genera-

[1]Revel, *Without Marx or Jesus.*

tion is unrealistic. It may well require many generations and take the form of a slow metamorphosis.

We have already described how, given the opportunity, children can become interested in human behavior and learn skills in problem solving. In this process of social learning, they begin to sense their own need for close ties with other people and the power of the peer group. At present, in most schools, this power is manifest in patterns of conformity. Physical size is equated with an individual pupil's power which can express itself negatively in bullying, or more acceptably in athletic success. In either case, a stereotype exists that largely precludes the questioning of group (classroom) values. The nonconformist in dress, social attitudes, activities, or interests is a "deviant" and may face rejection from his peers. Here lie the seeds for later mental health difficulties. The artistic, creative, sensitive, withdrawn, or independent child, the physically handicapped, small of stature or obese, may fail to find acceptance by his peers and drift into isolation, "illness," drugs or delinquency. Why wait until an alien environment identifies him as "ill" and refers him for treatment, when he is then identified as a patient, which further estranges him from his peers (and maybe his family) and reinforces his own negative self-image?

We have started with a consideration of the classroom rather than the home as a setting for social learning because the former is more available on a large scale. Obviously, the home and the school should be seen as complementary, and social learning if practiced by parents will reinforce similar experiences at school. The values of society at present would seem to favor a closed system for school-age children with the power and control largely invested in the parents and teachers. If, as seems possible, a slow process of democratization is visible in American society, then theoretically school teachers are more available for exposure to systems theory in their training than parents, who receive no formal training for parenthood, or systems theory applied to the family. Ironically, only those families judged to be "sick" are exposed to such a training through family therapy which usually leans heavily on a systems approach.

If the evolution toward open schools, which has already started, gains momentum, and learning as a social process ranks in importance with teaching formal subjects and memorizing subject matter, then the pupils of today will become the parents and teachers of tomorrow. This seems to me to be the only way in which a restructuring of society as an open system can occur. Existing systems, whether political, industrial, educational, recreational, racial, national, or family are so resistant to change that it is hard to visualize fundamental changes unless we start with the early development of the child.

Hitler may be an example of a change agent who affected dramatic changes in a comparatively short time. But his ideology was based on the abuse of power to achieve a "master race" and under his regime deviancy often resulted in death. Two-way communication, sharing of thoughts and feelings, shared decision making, social learning, and growth were totally unacceptable. The social, economic, and political forces at the time conspired to make the innate passivity of the masses an easy prey to dreams of world dominance and power. Is the current climate in the United States propitious for social change of a fundamentally different order?

I am advocating an entirely new approach to the problems of mental health without any claim to being original. And the changes effected by the field of applied behavioral science point in the direction of more open systems. Mental health is increasingly critical of certain aspects of the medical model, and is getting ever nearer to the consumer in his natural setting through the developing ideas of community psychiatry.

But the enormous potential of the peer group, demonstrated by living and learning experiences at school, is just beginning to have its advocates. When children and young adults have been educated in understanding the dynamics of behavior, of social, economic, and cultural factors in determining one's self-image, they will have the skills to help in the developing social systems and values that will enhance growth in the direction of health.

Given such an outcome or even some progress in that direction, we can only guess at how much of present-day "deviancy" will be seen to mask unsuspected potential for growth. Will school dropouts of today be seen as potential leaders of tomorrow? Will the nonconformist, the deviant, and the risk-taker be seen as symptoms of *our* social ineptitude and invoke a learning process, rather than be identified as "sick" and written off as unimportant?

Our vagueness in relation to health, compared with our interest in "sickness" as it exists at present, invites criticism, or even total rejection for being unrealistic. But this very uncertainty as to the future of education, and our resistance to embarking on the road to more flexible social systems jeopardizes further exploration into the unknown.

The hope is expressed that open systems will prepare children for the adult world so that responsibility for one's peers' peace of mind will not be burden, but a natural part of one's self-image, and will hold the same position in our future culture as material success and status do today. Only then can we expect the general population to understand and carry out some of the present-day expectations related to community psychiatry.

It may be that in this growth process psychiatry will lose much of its present-day importance. My hope is that mental health professionals will change with the times and find a valued place as facilitators in the new educational system, helping people to help themselves.

Index